BIG SOULS
MAKE BIG PROMISES

Reveal Hidden Personal & Family Dynamics to Unleash Your Heart

JOURNEY INTO THE HEART Vol. 1

SHAUNA CUCH

Speaker · Healer · Leader

Big Souls Make Big Promises:
Reveal Hidden Personal & Family Dynamics to Unleash Your Purpose

Copyright © 2020 by Shauna Cuch

RHG Media Productions
25495 Southwick Drive #103
Hayward, CA 94544.

IISBN 978-1-7361073-0-0 (paperback)
ISBN 978-1-7361073-1-7 (hardcover)

Visit us on line at www.YourPurposeDrivenPractice.com
Printed in the United States of America.

"The way you help heal the world is you go home and start with your own family."

— St. Mother Theresa

WHAT PEOPLE ARE SAYING

"*Big Souls Make Big Promises* is an extraordinary of healing methodology. This book will open your eyes to the vital importance of resolving intergenerational trauma. A five-star work!"
—Bridget Cook-Burch, New York Times Bestselling Author & Mentor

"This rich tapestry weaves the author's personal stories and diverse life experiences with practical case studies to offer the reader a taste of the divine connection that runs through us all. Well done!"
—Aeriol Ascher, MsD

"This book is a treasure of consciousness to embody our authentic Self."
—Sophie Roumeas - Therapist, Mindfulness Coach, Francophone author

"Your book is from the heart and reflects an honesty and a compassion rare in this world. Congratulations on a life well lived!!"
—Randall Tolpinrud, President, Pax Natura Foundation

"Shauna gives voice to that inner child we all have inside who desires to be loved, nurtured, and listened to as part of a family and the world we share."
—Dr Cheryl Lentz, TEDx Speaker & #1 International Best-selling Author

CONTENTS

ACKNOWLEDGEMENTS

I express my heartfelt gratitude to all my teachers and trainers that made a great impact on my life:

Francesca Mason Boring, who is dedicated to the integrity of this work. Her example and teachings have changed my life forever. She saw the gift in me and gave me the confidence to overcome my fears.

Kathleen McGarry, who introduced me to the beauty and wisdom of horses and how to honor and see them as my sages.

Alison Armstrong taught me so much more than "understanding men" and why women think men are misbehaving. She is a great example of how every word you say has a specific meaning and to stand by your word at all costs.

My wonderful parents, who did their best to live the life they believed was required of them. They gifted me with the experience of my abuse that made me who I am.

Our beautiful healing horses, Judy, Magic, Baby Girls, Sugar, Buffalo Joe, Rusty, and our amazing and majestic healer, Shadow. They have made a huge impact on raising consciousness. Also, my horse-whisperer son Jason who trains the horses to be gentle and reads them in a way that honors their empathic gifts and ability to heal.

And last but not least, I acknowledge my 11 extraordinary children who have allowed me to make mistakes in spite of my upbringing. They love and accept me for who I am and always show me respect and support in my journey.

—Shauna

MESSAGE FROM THE AUTHOR

W hile it took me sixty years to uncover the mystery, DNA Recoding in the form of a healing modality known as "Family Constellations" cleared deep, systemic trauma for me and my children. It also cleared profound unconscious, ancestral shame, as well as debilitating rage and oppression. What it created inside of me was freedom—freedom to live and fulfill my purpose and my passion.

Family Constellation work has been the most profound, vividly and dynamically healing work I have ever been a part of. I have seen more miracles involved with this work than with all other healing modalities combined. After so many decades of shame-filled silence, I could finally own my voice and self-expression. When you read on to hear my story, you will understand the significance of this.

The results have been stunning for me personally. After healing so profoundly, I discovered a deep sense of commitment to do this work as my life purpose. Now having facilitated hundreds of Constellations, it is my honor to watch the miracles unfold in the circle as the Seeker, like you, identifies patterns, makes discoveries, uncovers secrets, and especially heals the family DNA and clears the trauma and shame in the chair beside me. The Seeker quietly becomes a witness to the truth of their own ancestral patterns: a history that has been passed down intergenerationally, and most often unconsciously. The truth revealed is priceless. That truth sets them free, as it did for me.

Beyond immediate benefits, participants often call as much as a year later to inform me of the remarkable and positive changes they are continuing to see in their everyday lives, abundance, relationships and more.

So, I have a vital question for you:

If you could change your life right now, what would you want changed? What would you want to see for yourself or in the world would changed?

I believe this work will help heal the planet. And that is not an exaggeration, nor an understatement. I wrote this book to provide you with insight into this dynamic modality, to give you the courage to face your fears and any unhealthy patterns you may be ready to release and rewrite your past...and in doing so create a new future.

CHAPTER ONE

"But They Are So Well Behaved When He Spanks Them!"

The fact that you are reading this book tells me you are a big soul because this book is not for everyone. It is likely you realized at some point in time of your existence, just how much adversity you have faced and obstacles you have overcome. This tells me you must have made some noticeably big promises before you entered the world.

How do I know big souls make big promises? I grew up in a family with such big, dysfunctional patterns that it has taken a couple of generations of big souls to powerfully heal the backlash of trauma that had been going on for over a century, and perhaps even further back. The dysfunction was so great and the story so unique that I was told HBO's *Big Love* series was based on a portion of mine and my son's early personal stories. I did win a Mother of the Year award from the governor of the state of Utah--that is until they discovered that I was one of four wives in a polygamist relationship.

But it didn't start there.

It was not an accident that I arrived at one of the most difficult times possible for my parents. In 1952, I was born in a century-old house with fourteen rooms that were in constant need of repair. Raised in polygamy, my father married three wives. My mother was his third wife, and she gave birth to ten girls and three boys. I was her tenth child and my dad's twenty-ninth child. Raised in polygamy, my mother would eventually have thirteen children of her own.

Mom only nursed her babies to keep from getting pregnant, it was her only form of birth control. At nine months, she discovered she was pregnant once again with her eleventh baby. Rather than communicate to me soul to soul that she no longer wanted to nurse me, instead she did what became the normal. In a cold, resentful tone, she turned me over to my dad to shut down my pleading cries, despite the fact that I was only begging for nurturing love and affection. Dad's method, "children were to be seen, and not heard" resulted in beatings. Every time I let out a cry, my pleas were returned with a continuous resounding blow to my head, face, or upper body. Finally, I would stop in sheer exhaustion, only to start again whenever he came around again. A one-time beating worked for my older sisters, but for my old soul, I did not give up easily. What ensued was an inner battle with the deep need to be heard.

My older sisters were taught by my mother, "If you change and feed Shauna and she still cries, put her in her crib. She is just spoiled." That isolation became my deepest fear. I could disassociate from the beatings, but to be confined in that crib upstairs away from the other children...unseen and unheard for hours with no way out, that is where I lost my voice. Instead of a normal baby's needs being met, it was ingrained within me by nine months old that I deserved to be punished for self-expression.

As I grew into a toddler, my determination to be heard at all cost became my personality. I developed a shrill, loud voice according to my mom's looks even when I squealed with delight as I played.

"Shauna, keep it down!" she would order harshly, as she looked over her shoulders annoyed. Her words and example became the mainstream thinking amongst my siblings.

"Mom, Shauna is throwing a fit again! She won't stop crying." they complained.

"Shut her in her room until she behaves!"

It was as though I had to defend my right to exist to everyone, from the younger to the older siblings who were my caregivers. I also learned that love had conditions. I believed that I was unworthy to be loved unless my behavior was perfect and my voice silent and unexpressed.

Unbeknownst to me, I inherited my mother's suppressed rage in the womb. I became more and more suppressed as my will to be heard shrunk, creating an altered personality. **I had lost my authentic voice**, and what would have been apparent to a psychologist was just annoying to others. **I was either silent or spoke out of turn. I was not even conscious of the lashing out that would occur underneath. It all stemmed from hidden fear that something was wrong with me. I unconsciously created a rebel inside.** That rebel was a self-fulfilling prophecy. It blurted out for people to witness my outbursts and to fulfill my fears of "I am not lovable if I speak."

Only ten of my dad's thirty-three children lived with us. Our home was filled from top to bottom, as my mom cared for seven other children to earn money. At the same time, my two-year-old sister was hospitalized for eight months with polio. Mom also took in boarders that she had to feed in the rooms above us. In our culture, the women had to turn their money over to their husbands. Dad never left her much allowance to feed us all, so macaroni and tomato sauce was the staple at the time.

Our family did not belong to any specific group of polygamists. Unlike the Kingston's, Allred's, FLDS and others, we were called independents. In other words, we no longer followed a man who claimed to be a prophet. Independent of any leader, our group of about a thousand fit somewhat into the mainstream of life in the outside world—but only somewhat. When I went to public school, those differences quickly became clear to me. The poverty was obvious; I have no memory of getting new clothes. Like other polygamists in the state, however, we had to stay quiet about our lifestyle and beliefs or my parents could be arrested and taken from us. As a family, we lived with that fear every day.

Still, I did not feel like I belonged at home, either. I felt awkwardly different than most of my mom's younger children. They all had big brown eyes like Mom, while mine were greenish-blue. Two sisters just older than me both had thick, curly hair, while mine was thin and wispy, making my ears poke out. Those sisters were very smart; everyone listened to them. I on the other hand, felt bad and wrong the limited times I did speak for myself. Inside, however, I was unaware of the rebellious spirit I had cultivated. I just kept it tucked up inside of me along with the hidden fear for the most part. With all my fears so deeply hidden and finally out of the confinement of the crib, I would never allow anyone to fit me into their idea of me. The challenge was that I did not know who I was, and I had not received validation nor nurturing from my mother, and certainly not from my father.

My dad, a big burly man with a booming voice; moved away from our home to a ranch where there was no room for the rest of us. Whenever he came to visit us on occasion throughout the month, I was terrified of him and that thunderous voice. It always seemed raised in anger and frustration, so the moment I heard it, I would find a place to hide. His temper was legendary and his authority absolute, until he left again. I did not understand why I was so afraid of men; I had suppressed the memory of the spankings and beatings. **I was even scared of men who were gentle and considerate.**

"Mom, I don't like it when Dad spanks the babies when they cry," my older sister whimpered to our mom with tears streaming down her face as she listened to her little sister screaming.

"Yes, I know, dear," replied Mom calmly, despite the chaos. "But they are so well behaved after he does it." Her words sent a chill down my sister's spine.

Mom was shut down emotionally from her own childhood abuse. Instead, she quietly seethed around the edges. She did not want to allow strong emotions to surface around her children. She'd been taught by her own father never to show when she was being upset or any kind of emotion in front of the children or "you set a bad example." That's why when she became angry or had enough of us whining, she handed us over to Dad.

When I turned seven years old, we were all traumatized when my father was arrested for polygamy and sent to prison. It had been our worst fear. When it was clear his sentence would be lengthy, he was anxious for visitors. In the past, Dad had his favorites, and I knew I was not one of them. For the first time, when we went to visit him, he treated me kindly when we arrived, and I was astonished, and it melted my heart. He wrinkled his nose when he smiled, mimicking my face and calling me "Pinkie". For those four years, I saw the affectionate side of him. It was easy to replace the blustering, terrifying, angry man with this kind one I'd always wanted. It was my fantasy. I suppressed any unpleasant memory from my mind and conveniently replaced it with my dad's now kind glances and smiles across the table from him in prison.

While he was in prison, I was often alone, the little forest imp, with an affinity for birds and freedom. Daily I was awash in a deep love of nature, gentleness, natural communication with my spirit guides who were dear to me, and I had a great love for other people. I grew deeply spiritual, and often spoke with my angels and saw things that other people did not always see.

In relationships, however, I operated in complete and total survival mode from my limbic brain. With no one to trust, I embodied the belief that I was not lovable. This belief isolated me from connecting with others. Rarely did I ever lose my temper, but when I did, LOOK OUT! I did not care what happened; I felt like I had to fight with every ounce of my being. After all, I was fighting for survival and for my freedom. I did not understand safety except to hide and isolate. I did not understand my hunger for freedom but if I felt controlled, confined or unloved I would fight to be among the fittest.

Since I was not the oldest, nor the youngest, eventually there was not much I feared. As the years progressed, **I stopped being quiet and my behaviors swung to the other side of the pendulum. I became loud, pushy, and self-serving. My behavior was often unpredictable.** Even though I loved my sisters and mothers, unconsciously they symbolized the crib in all of its confinement. As I grew older, I began getting along much better with males. I never seemed to be able to trust females. That feeling would only worsen.

CHAPTER TWO

A Live Bobcat in the Tent

One day after our father was finally released from prison, he took all the children from our families camping that were not yet married. We went high up into the mountains where no one could interfere with our celebration or throw him back in prison. I was ten years old at the time and seven of us young girls slept in a big army tent together. After a late, celebratory night around the campfire, an older sister from my other mother and I were being lazy and sleeping in. I awoke to her berating me.

"You're stealing my blankets!" she bellowed as she yanked the heavy quilted material from me. It was cold inside that tent in the mountains, and I glared at her, unhappy to be awakened so rudely. I grabbed the hem of the fabric and yanked them back off her.

"These are not your blankets; they are Mom's!" I retorted

"I am your elder!" she shot back, using a term bandied about in our family and culture quite profusely. Everything was always about authority and control. If you were male or if you were older, you always were supposed to have authority. "You must do as I say," she continued, "so give me the blanket." Violently she tried to tug at them again, but I held on tight, being three years younger notwithstanding.

"YOU ARE NOT THE BOSS OF ME!" I shrieked. I did not care that she was much bigger and older than me. I was not having it. The tussling suddenly got out of hand. She started punching me and calling me names. In retaliation, I reached up and grabbed her long hair that had spilled loose onto my face. She was hurting, she pivoted from pummeling my body to punching me in the nose and my face. It hurt so bad; yet I was seeing red by then. I grabbed another lock of hair and the carnage only escalated.

Alerted by the screams, Dad neared our tent to see it violently wobbling back and forth. When he saw long strands of hair flying out of the tent's entrance, he thought we were under attack. Our father raced in to rescue us only to find his two innocent girls tussling for life. He ordered us out of the tent and threw a bucket of cold water on the two of us. As we sputtered, dripping, he cried, "Can't you girls get along? You scared me half to death. I thought a bobcat was in your tent!"

Therefore, even my older sisters said they feared me, though I was rarely angry. Once attacked, adrenaline would surge, and I would fight to the end. I felt no pain when experiencing rage and this instinctive fight for survival.

Fortunately, I got better at suppressing that rage as I got older. I was not as defensive, and I was able to make friends in junior high and high school. **Even if deep down I did not feel lovable, I was fortunate to learn that I was likeable outside of my family and that I had nothing to prove.**

Now that Dad was home, he would spend a week at each wife's house. We knew when it was Dad's turn with Mom. She would always have us set the table up just for Dad and the older boys if they were home. Everything had to be exactly right, or Dad would make a stink about it. He liked to be fussed over. Mom would fuss over him as he liked, but since his return from prison I saw a coolness behind her eyes. She had handled everything without him while he was gone. **Quietly I realized she did not really need him, and I was not sure she wanted him, either.**

What my experience taught me was that young girls were to allow men dominion over their personal space, and their lives. This patriarchal system can possibly lead to sexual and physical abuse on many levels. The men could justify it and the women were taught from youth to be submissive to men. That was the case in our home where unconscious, inappropriate behaviors took place. Intentional or not, they happened, nevertheless. In our family, my dad crossed that line several times with his temper and other inappropriate behavior when his daughters matured.

My brother crossed that line with my sister who was maturing. When she reported an incident to my mom, our mother simply explained, "That is how men are," as she gave her the birds and bees speech. Mom taught us that we must submit to our father and our husband at all cost. It was our way, and more importantly, it was "the way" in our religion. Even though she was very smart, secretly wanted a career and never wanted a large family, she did it all for "the religion."

I was sitting in our Sunday School one day at home at the age of six. I raised my hand with a burning question.

"Why do the boys get all the privileges over the girls in our family?" I was tired of giving up my chair to my brothers and having to sit on the floor, among other things.

"A woman falls under the umbrella of her father and then her husband," Mom replied coolly. "The men are responsible for your salvation; he is your path to get into the kingdom of God. If a woman chooses to leave her husband, then she must leave her children with him because she is in rebellion and the children belong to the Patriarch."

CHAPTER THREE

Rebellion ~ Love ~ Freedom

"**M**om, I know who I am going to marry!" my 14-year-old self-proclaimed loudly to my mother. She was watching her favorite Loretta Young Show on TV. Blurting out that way was the only way I could get her attention.

She quickly shot me a look of disapproval and looked back at her show. "Why on earth would you even speak about marriage at your age?" she said sternly. "Don't even think about boys until you're sixteen, let alone marriage."

The rule in our house was very firm. You could not date until you were sixteen. Then your suitor must ask your dad's permission to even date you. Our clan did not believe in arranged marriages, but if the father approved, then he would come ask you if you were interested in that man. This was an especially good thing if the man courting you was already married. That way, your dad could screen him for you before the man approached you. My parents were extremely strict about not getting married until you were seventeen.

I had yet to follow the strict rules my parents imposed on us. I managed to get around all that, I was sneaking out to date at fourteen. Struggling with learning challenges at school, I fell in love with a cowboy. **Lynn was part of our culture, so he understood our beliefs and had grown up in polygamy as**

well. By the time I turned sixteen, he proposed, and I was more than willing to ditch tenth grade and dive into marriage with a man more than five years older than me. My mom was against marrying that young, but Lynn managed to get permission from my dad. My mother would not speak to me for months while I planned and paid for my own wedding. It was only the day before the wedding when she finally faced the fact that I was going ahead with it that she asked if she could help.

The day of my wedding, I thought I was in paradise. I was with the man I loved, and I was free from school. I also thought, wrongly, that I was free of all the restrictions, controls, and manipulations that I faced in my childhood home.

Delighted to be married, I busied myself as a homemaker, but I was headstrong, and my husband seemed to know I had my limits. Nine months later, we brought a child into the world and I loved him the way I felt he should be loved. I nursed my babies on demand; I would never put them in a crib. I surrounded them in educational toys to make learning fun.

Unfortunately, my husband's strict ideas on discipline triggered all kinds of emotions inside my body that I did not understand. I struggled horrifically if my husband insisted, I let our babies cry, and especially if he lost his temper at the children. **We began to fight a lot in front of our kids. The more I tried to stop him from his way of discipline, the worse he became. It seemed he could tell that I was triggered, and he used that to flex his muscles.** He dug in his heels. The triggers were even worse than my childhood trauma because even as an adult, I felt powerless to stop it. Lynn was the man of the family. I was supposed to be obedient and defer to my husband now. I felt responsible and guilty when his temper got the better of him at times with his children. Despite all of this, I felt the pressure of building a bridge of love with the children towards their dad, temper and all. I softened everything that I could, and I would take all the blame so they wouldn't hold resentment against their father. I was able to make our home a safe place. . . most of the time.

I quickly became attuned to their energy fields and their suffering. This gave me a deep love for healing and supporting emotional and spiritual growth in my children and others. Like the child spirit in the woods, but now as a grown woman I had a powerful conduit of knowing. My connection to Spirit grew strong and vital. I became not only conscious of the energy of others, but I was also able to see others' true potential for greatness.

The one good thing that came from trying to resolve all this conflict was that as my intuition grew, I learned how repressed emotions cause illness. After discovering a book called *Messages of the Body*, by Michael Lincoln, **I learned early on that the ultimate cause for most sickness or disease was stuck, blocked, unresolved or unclaimed emotions. I didn't know it at the time, but this knowledge would be a catalyst for everything that came after.**

CHAPTER FOUR

The Deepest and Most Difficult Growth Imaginable

When I was pregnant with my seventh baby, my husband was approached by a family friend to marry his daughter. She was young and beautiful. Unlike my mother, I wore all my emotions on my sleeves. I agreed to the marriage because that was where my guidance told me my most growth would be, Sure enough! I really struggled with jealousies over this beautiful girl to the point that one evening I was so upset that I rode the car to a Mormon church parking lot. There in the privacy of the car, sobbed within what felt a life's breath. I cried so hard; my belly ached.

After arriving home, my face red and swollen, I'd gone to bed. I was surprised to be awakened early morning in labor just as the birds came out to awaken me. I was two weeks early. I did not realize it at the time, but that child had to suffer that pain along with me. He was very adult and mature as a toddler.

Several years later, my husband's other wife had two sisters that wanted to join our family. By then I had conquered my jealousies and learned to accept the polygamous lifestyle. After we all agreed, he set about marrying two more, we lived together splitting his time between all of us. I worked vigorously to live unitedly and be fair. However, anytime a woman has to share a man with other women, it's very difficult to feel like anything was fair.

I strived to be truly kind to my sister-wives because they became important to me. So did their children, especially as my children's siblings, I loved them very much.

For his part, Lynn experienced difficulties not allowing his insecurities to get the best of him. The more confident and powerful my relationship with Creator became, the more insecure he felt, even though I gave him plenty of attention. Whenever I turned my energy to my children and into my spiritual life, his insecurities flared. I did my best to be happy and my connection to Spirit was my sustaining grace through three more children.

As my confidence in myself and my mothering grew, the feminine power became threatening to Lynn, as it often does to men in patriarchal religious societies. I was out from under his control, I had found my peace from within. Unfortunately, everything I worked hard to build would all come tumbling down when my husband's health began to quickly decline because of diabetes.

Lynn had been extremely fit and healthy when I first met him, but his eating habits were terrible. He did not believe that what you ate had anything to do with your health. Even though I intuitively understood and tried to help him through the years, it took its toll.

Life as we knew it came to a crashing halt when my husband died at forty-nine years old, leaving behind four wives and seventeen children. With my six children still living in my home, I became their father, mother, and provider with only a tenth-grade education.

In time, I made another attempt at plural marriage. This time instead of being the first wife, I became Michael's fourth wife. I had gained a lot of confidence from standing up to my abusive late husband, so I was no longer a pushover. Very quickly, that did not settle well with Michael. In addition, he could not hold down a job, and clearly had mother issues. Eventually, it was his untrue belief that a woman could and should *not* receive revelation for her family that was the last straw. Revelation was "only the man's place" in his eyes, even though I was now receiving it in my daily life. After seven years of trying to convince me that I was out of line, our family split apart as he left all of us to live alone.

I felt I had learned all I could from this lifestyle, but I still had children at home to raise. After another failed marriage, this time outside of polygamy, I knew I had to do something drastically different.

CHAPTER FIVE

Learning to Trust My Intuition

I had never worked outside of the home before, so I did what I do best. Brainstorming on my domestic skills, I started a catering business named Panache that took off after getting several catering gigs for the Utah Olympics.

Shortly after I got a call from the manager of the hottest venue in town with three banquet rooms wanting me to be the exclusive caterer. Out of all the companies she watched during the Olympics, she chose mine.

I was surprised because I had never catered before now and my main competitors had been in business for over twenty-five years! I knew one example of our charm was including fresh flowers at the tables to show the public that I cared about them. Other caterers eventually gave the same service, but I set the standard because they were not an upgrade; they were our standard.

That is when she hit me with the terms of her offer. "The landlord will insist that you take on the wine bar, café, and restaurant along with it. They are in the red $360,000 because they are landlords and they know nothing about the food business." She held her breath for a minute to see my reaction.

I had to go home and pray about it. It seemed like a lot for someone with no experience in food service industry. Also, this was still Utah, and I was worried because many of the citizens did not drink, much less specialized wines.

I went home, got my answer, and cried for the next two weeks. The thought of leaving my children for the first time in my life broke my heart. Even my catering kitchen had previously been built on my property, so I was only a sidewalk away from my house. This was downtown, an hour away from home. Still, listening to the Spirit I knew I was to take this challenge on.

Despite having absolutely no experience, in two years I turned a profit. I won many awards for my catering and wine bar and was written up in *Sky West Magazine* as the best wine bar in Utah and Ted Scheffler wrote two raving reviews about my Soirée wine tasting dinners.

I climbed to the top quickly, and soon I was supervising eighty employees. After five years, in a pattern of fear of success, just as I crossed from the red to profitable, I lost everything overnight: my million-dollar home, my land, and my business. I then beat myself up emotionally for what I kept creating, believing I was stupid or crazy. It was time; I was destined to discover my truth. My only consolation was knowing that food service was not my path.

One of my first customers at the wine bar eventually became my fourth husband, Frank. Full-blooded Native American, I felt he was one of the reasons that I landed that venue. We were destined to meet, and he became the one that by fate, led me to my true path of healing. Frank and I eventually married and moved to the Native American reservation. My son Jason built us a house on Frank's forty acres with the help of other family members. Because of my business expertise, I was hired by the tribe as a business consultant and opened a new restaurant and upgraded their grocery store in a short-term project.

Frank's son had been raising American Paint horses on the reservation land. However, he no longer wanted the hassle of the animals, so he gave all the horses to his dad. Despite my busy schedule, nearly every day I felt compelled to go out and connect with these beautiful creatures. Frank gave me a horse of my own, Baby Girl.

As our connection grew, **I came to discover the amazing ability horses have to read human emotions. After my project was over, I stepped away from the consulting. It did not take me long to realize that my gift of healing could partner with horses to help release deep pain and trauma.**

One day my equine therapy trainer could feel tension that was happening between Frank and me. He was feeling very territorial with her staying at our home. The trainer suggested that we should go out and work out our disagreement with the horses. I immediate went outside and began talking to Baby Girl and Shadow about our disagreement. Frank walked up in front of me, and barked, "What!"

Just then, Baby Girl snapped at him with her teeth.

"Stop being mean!" he barked again.

Suddenly Shadow our most gentle horse, snapped at him with his teeth.

"STOP THAT!" he yelled, and suddenly he stopped and began to laugh. We both realized the horses were mirroring his behavior and attitude towards me. Surprisingly, that brought resolve. Frank was able to calm down and we were able to communicate more effectively with each other for a time.

Frank was constantly telling me his people, the Ute tribe, needed healing. This was true as they had experienced deep trauma. Still, we were both to discover, in fact, that it was *Frank* that deserved healing. It did not take me long to realize Frank had dysfunctional mother issues that eventually took their toll on any relationship he had. What hurt my heart to witness was that I could clearly see how his resulting patterns were keeping him from self-love. This was his major struggle. At the time, I did not realize it reflected my own trauma.

I was willing to work ridiculously hard for both love and money, but it never turned out well. I did not realize that I was running a pattern. On a very deep level, I had been emotionally and physically abused. I didn't realize my hidden shadow had shut out any memory of my childhood in order to survive it—yet unconsciously as an adult, the shame of it was running my life! Love and abundance have similar vibrations, and I could not succeed at either one.

In addition, I did not know how to stand up to a man powerfully without defending and explaining. Their criticism triggered my inner story that I was unlovable. I would defend myself, feel disempowered, and try to fix or change myself. I would lose myself in nurturing my spouse to fix him so he could love me.

I witnessed Frank showing everyone else respect in public, yet many times as soon as we walked into our home, his disrespectful comments started for no apparent reason. I knew better than to react or respond. He was deeply traumatized from his mother's suicide. I knew berating me is what he saw his mother do. I was the shadow transmuting expert for everyone else, I was psychic, I was familiar with his pattern. Yet I could not help this body response I had to his criticism. Deep down, I felt it was true so I would try harder to fix me so I could be lovable.

I was such a lover of men, though, that I even became certified by Alison Armstrong to teach "Understanding Men," a course that helps women understand the differences and dynamics of how differently men think and operate from women. It helped me to understand things intellectually, but it did not break the pattern I had been living.

CHAPTER SIX

I Found My Truth and Became Whole

One day, I heard about a healing symposium being held in Texas by two facilitators from Australia who used horses in their healing work. After listening to their testimonial about their work, I was astounded and felt inspired to attend. It called to me on a very deep level. I had been helping to heal Native American families with horses on my husband's reservation for six years and had found it extremely effective. **Could Family Constellations add to the work I was doing to make it even more effective? I researched it and found this modality was mainstream in thirty countries, even though America was not as quick to turn to natural methods of healing trauma.**

I told my husband about the event right away. "I really feel called to go to Texas to this horse symposium and learn some new methods of healing. Do you want to go with me?" I asked.

"No," he quipped impatiently. "Someone has to stay home with the horses. Can't you just stay home for once?"

"Can you hire the neighbor boy to do that?" I suggested, knowing he always felt abandoned when I would leave. We had led an active life since we had met, but ever since we moved on to his people's reservation, he never wanted to travel.

"No!" he growled. "And I am not paying for it. You will have to come up with the money yourself."

"I will earn my own way, don't worry," I said quickly, surprised at my excitement and the call within me I felt to go. I signed up for all ten days. This event was a huge turning point in my life. In the Family Constellation session, we all sat in chairs around the corral. The facilitator said she would show us the method rather than explain it. Suddenly, she turned to me.

"Would you like to go in with the horses?"

"Sure!" I jumped up quickly and walked into the corral. She asked me a few questions, and I told her I had learned recently of my abuse and neglect as an infant by my parents.

She had me choose one Representative from the participants for my dad and one for my mom. Then she had me sit in a chair and brought over one of the horses.

"This horse represents you as a baby."

It was fascinating to watch because my abuse as an infant started when my mom found out she was pregnant with another child when I was only nine months old. She did not want to nurse me after that, so every time I cried, she turned me over to Dad. He took on the challenge to shut me down by slapping me till I was too exhausted to cry, yet I never stopped trying to be heard.

Now, this horse that was representing me put her nose in my chest area. It took me a while to realize she was acting as if she was nibbling at my breasts, because that is where it all started.

The facilitator asked the Representative of my mom how she was doing. The woman held her stomach and said she was sick and wanted nothing to do with me. I was my mom's tenth child, and she had told us many times she only wanted four children but had more for the sake of her religion. The facilitator instructed me to go up and talk to my mom, and she put us through a healing process by replacing the story with truth and a powerful statement of acknowledgement and forgiveness.

After the facilitator worked with us, my mother's Representative ended up hugging me and telling me she was sorry, and that she loved me very much.

I went over to my dad's Representative, and after the facilitator worked with us, she asked him if he wanted to hug me. He said to me, "Everything in my body wants to give you a hug, but I keep getting told to just give you respect."

Something inside of me shifted in that comment. I suddenly felt I was worthy of the respect I could never get from a man! This changed me in a way that I cannot explain, but it would later show up powerfully in the way I would hold myself and take responsibility for myself.

Before I left the symposium, I did another Constellation that was very deep that involved my older siblings who had confined me to a crib for my "bad behavior" of crying. I witnessed my simple desires to be fed and held. I also witnessed how much responsibility for me was placed on them by a mother who felt overwhelmed with her own children.

That, too, was powerfully healing for me. I had not been a bad or unlovable child. I had been born into an exceedingly difficult situation that was stressful for everyone around me who took it out on me. I left the symposium with new eyes to see my life, and new energy to consciously be aware of my feelings.

When I arrived home to settle into my routine, my husband was cross with me for being gone, because he felt abandoned. He threw out an immediate, blatant criticism toward me. For the first time, I did not feel hurt or react.

This time as I observed him running this pattern, I noticed an electrifying change within my body. I felt a personal power surge into my breast as I looked him in the eyes.

"Thank you for sharing," I responded calmly. "I realize I created this pattern from the past because I thought I was broken. I understand now that I am not broken, and I would appreciate you showing me some respect."

His jaw dropped, and he just glared at me, not knowing what to say. I felt three feet taller as I looked at him lovingly and left the room without fighting and went about my work. I was equally shocked, as I had been trying for years to stand up to any man without being rebellious or defensive. **In deep gratitude for the healing I experienced, I realized it had shown me that I was whole again.**

I knew then that this Constellation work, and the work with horses, was the most powerful healing work I had ever experienced in all my training. I had never stood both compassionate and firm in my boundaries since we had been married, but something physical had shifted inside of me—in my body, in my brain, and in my energy field. Of course, my husband felt it and was astonished.

CHAPTER SEVEN

Clearing the Shackles of Ancestral DNA

I discovered through this healing work that all emotional trauma from our ancestors and ourselves becomes stored. This negative energy remains stuck, and even gets passed down through patterns and behaviors to our descendants. Although I had done a considerable amount of energy work before this, I couldn't help but see how effectively Family Constellations worked on an energetic level to address where the trauma started in the first place, and relieve the symptoms showing up in the physical, mental, emotional, and spiritual bodies of later generations.

I had inherited energetic information from past trauma and oppression in my polygamist ancestors and was living their patterns. Not only that, I was passing this energy on, including my own added traumas, to my children without realizing it. My husband at the time, from his tribal background, was doing the same to his children.

When I could see the power to stop, shift, and change the energy and behaviors, that's when I knew I had to learn this modality thoroughly, and get it out into the world. Family Constellations gifted me with a deep awareness that sent me on a huge awakening journey to step into my own power...and discover my own self-love. After what I had been through, this was transformative for me.

I inquired regarding training in Family Constellations I signed up with a Shoshone woman named Francesca Mason Boring. She did not utilize horses, only people in her Constellation training, but I learned all she had to teach me during that time. Through her work, I realized that whether a facilitator utilized horses or not, Constellations remained very powerful and effective. Francesca authored several books on the method. I read each of them before I came to her training, and then invested time and money to become certified in both beginning and advanced training.

Every time I facilitated Constellations at my training with Francesca, I felt the sacredness of the work. being done there. My instructor pulled me aside a few times and told me, "Shauna, you are a gift to the circle." At the time, I did not know what she meant. All I knew was that I was seeing, feeling, experiencing the deeper truth from beyond.

During advanced training, we were instructed to do a Constellation in peer groups on our business model. When my turn came, my Representative in the circle felt her stomach and said, "I feel like I have a baby in my stomach!" Suddenly I felt movement in *my* stomach. I knew that it was movement from the work I had recently been doing. What was interesting was recognizing that my hidden fear and rage shadow from being shut down, neglected, and abused as a young child was surfacing.

I allowed myself to feel it but didn't act on it. I had a strong conviction that this was not the appropriate time or place to do a personal Constellation. The trainees saw the look on my face, however, and rushed over to get Francesca. When she came over to the circle of truth, she took one look at me and embraced me.

"What are you feeling, Shauna?" she asked, concerned.

"I am feeling movement in my stomach from the unexpressed rage of an angry inner child that is finally surfacing.

She is ready to be released, but I don't feel this business Constellation training is the time or place for it."

"No, it is not," replied Francesca firmly. Still, she grabbed me and held me tight, whispering, "Tell the child you have a voice and you *will* be heard, but now is not the time."

I did as she instructed, and while she was still holding me close to her, I whispered to Francesca what I was experiencing, and I recently had an awareness that this hidden shadow had actually altered or caused a split personality.

"That may be the case," she agreed, "it is not uncommon when someone has severe childhood trauma to have voices surface in whatever way they can to find resolution."

As Francesca was embracing my fear-filled self, she noticed I was admiring her beautiful necklace. It was delicate yet elaborate, with several tiny buffalos carved in bone interlaced with turquoise. To my surprise, she suddenly removed her necklace and placed it around my neck. She then told me again in front of the others, "Shauna, the buffalo medicine is powerful in this work. You are a gift to the circle. Call upon the buffalo medicine anytime during this work." She had placed me in the care of the White Buffalo, a powerful healing Spirit in Native American cosmology.

Now, I was more than surprised; I felt deeply honored by her expression. In fact, even though I was still unsure what it meant at the time, I would soon discover that she saw my gifts and commitment to the work. Learning how to facilitate Family Constellations was actually the path to fulfilling my sacred commitments and big promises—and to help others fulfill theirs, too.

From my first Constellation to the many weeks and months of doing Constellations and shadow work I did during my training as a facilitator, I was able to better serve others because I dealt with my own shadows and ancestral trauma.

I feel this is an important point: I discovered from my own experience that any energy worker who has not done their personal deeper shadow work is more apt to either project their own stories, trigger, or download soul wounds. After successfully facilitating Family Constellations for a number of years, I also train *facilitators* to do this deep inner work in order to spread this work in a healthy manner for years to come.

My life is not the same. I am not the same person trained as an infant to submit to a man's patriarchal authority. I am living my life powerfully, doing what I love, and gifting this amazing work to those who are stuck in a loop of negativity, trauma, or family patterns and want to find freedom to live their truth, find their purpose, and uncover their gifts to share with the world.

The beautiful truth is that I have no interest in fixing anyone. Instead, what I love is that this method helps you see for yourself what your patterns are, and where they come from, and how speaking the truth in the Constellation circle brings healing energetically without you even realizing it until it shows up physically. The amazing result is it not only affects everyone you're in contact with, but all your ancestors and your children who may have been impacted by your generational pattern.

The healing done in the circle causes a movement of the soul and continues to heal where love and connection were lost. With ancestral Constellations, you'll notice small changes for up to a year, and it just keeps going.

Continued Constellations help release more patterns, habits, thoughts, and unhealthy behaviors. In the book entitled *13 Grandmothers Counsel the World*, these globally renowned healers made a profound statement: "Man must heal four generations in order to heal the Earth." I have recognized in this work that if a person heals all four biological grandparents, they are cleared from the shackles of ancestral DNA that causes the fractions in the family system that were haunting them physically and emotionally.

What is wonderful for me to witness is how this unfolds in the lives of participants. Many come to me who are searching for a way to fulfill their purpose in life, and what I have discovered is first, they get to uncover and release their untold stories they have inherited and reveal their truth so they feel empowered to actually own their gifts. Many of my participants who have done their ancestral work faithfully have uncovered their true spiritual gifts and are now contributing powerfully to the healing of the planet.

I'm also excited about the growing community of like-hearted people who understand the vital importance of doing Constellation work to bring light and love to their shadows. The Constellation community is very close to one another because we do the work as a whole, so each individual has great support when they need it.

I personally believe that the participants of the Constellation work are big souls who have made big promises. Whatever shows up in the circle is what they were carrying in their energy field and is often a soul wound of their ancestors and most likely something they obviously made a promise to heal. If nothing else, Constellations provide a way for us to experience the innate healing ability that resides within us all without exception. Each of us can participate actively in the healing of our families, and thus our world, by opening our perceptions and expanding our knowledge. We can set healthy boundaries and take back and own the responsibility that is ours and give back what does not belong to us. In this way, we alleviate suffering, and can bring to the world healthy individuals to lead, grow, and work more positively and effectively together.

I learned from all my experience that your shadow is never more powerful than your light. I was blessed with extreme faith, joy, and tenacity to match my shadow. Now my vibration of creation is amazing!

I invite you to read further. Explore the case studies. Compare some of the patterns in which you may have been stuck, or where loved ones have seemed stuck. Now is your time, like me, to claim your life back. It is your destiny, and now it's absolutely possible.

CHAPTER EIGHT

Introduction to Family Constellation Work

I f you could change your life right now, what about yourself and what in the world would you change?

Most people would say they would want to change their relationships. They want to change relationships in their family, relationships with themselves and relationships with abundance.

Family systems are all about relationships and the way in which we relate to one another in our connections and the energy in which we hold ourselves. However, family systems are so much more than groups of people who share the same genes or even the same address. We all look to our family as a source of love and support, but conflict can result as part of family life, and traumas can develop.

Some conflict is inherent in any relationship. However, trauma in families can create long-term issues if not addressed properly. These can include addictions, physical abuse, mental and physical illnesses, sexual abuse, marital and sibling issues, and more. It's been scientifically proven that patterns and trauma can be passed down from generation to generation. (Documentary: *Ghost in you Genes*)

What if you had the ability to finally heal yourself and the current issues you are facing in your life? Now imagine that by doing so, you are able to affect generations forward and back through your healing. What if you had the ability, and opportunity to clear generations of family trauma?

I ask you to imagine that you do, indeed, have the ability to create this powerful change. In fact, I am so excited to share with you that it is possible through the Constellation methodology.

The Constellation Methodology uses the Systemic Knowing Field to reveal unresolved traumas in the lives of individuals and their previous family members in subsequent and current generations. We are a walking history book, holding passed down traumas become blocks to our true nature in living as free individuals and allowing for our highest possible journey, choices, and alignment to our spiritual missions. Once the traumas are known, a space of truth is orchestrated where emotions can be safely released, dissolving what some may call ancestral karma.

Whatever you might call it, Neurobiologist Kerry Ressler's study with rats and cherry blossoms on the mechanisms of fear acquisition. Suggesting epigenetic inheritance rather than environment and that trauma and disease are passed down in as many as six generations. Constellation methodology is a safe space to release the stagnant, unhealthy energy of grief, trauma, depression, negativity, stress, anxiety, and disconnection from Source.

In the pages to come, we will combine science, spirituality, energy, medicine, and the Knowing Field to explore various obstacles that threaten our happiness and health – along with the understanding that there are now developed techniques to heal our wounds and release our traumas.

The purpose of Family Constellation work is to heal disruptions caused from pain or trauma somewhere in your ancestral line. These disruptions may become systemic by showing up in a consistent, continuous, and dysfunctional way. This inter-generational behavior then becomes imprinted for generations, creating emotional blocks, accidents, and unhealthy family patterns.

This pattern becomes embedded in our DNA, which is inherited mentally, physically, and emotionally. The pattern is unique to each person and causes a disconnect from love that disrupts our self-expression and authentic nature. These incompletions are passed on until someone takes the necessary steps to find resolve that helps ancestors rest in peace. Parents powerfully discover that harmony, love, and connection is a gift they can pass on to children and grandchildren after doing this work. Family Constellations Create Healthy Reconnections. Having the opportunity to see and experience previously unconscious ancestral patterns will show you a bigger picture and remove your judgements of yourself and others, while creating conscious compassion and love. As a participant, you are able to let go of expectations of parents and other parental figures and let go of old patterns that once

perhaps dominated your life. You are able to take precious responsibility for your present and future.

The work also sets boundaries for children so parents can be parents, and children can be children, and the result is a powerful self-sovereignty for each member of the family, along with the sacred power in honoring all relationships.

CHAPTER NINE

It Seems Magical ~ How Does a Constellation Work?

An unresolved ancestral issue leaves a family imprint or pattern that you find yourself engaging in which you devote no conscious attention. You just do it. Repetitions of that behavior create an entire lifestyle, whether positive or negative.

To change an unconscious behavior, conventional thought is that you have to apply personal discipline. Willpower. Determination. Frank Outlaw, the late president of Bi-Lo Stores once shared some oft-quoted advise: "Watch your thoughts, they become words; watch your words, they become actions; watch your actions, they become habits; watch your habits, they become character; watch your character, for it becomes your destiny."

Sounds great, doesn't it? However, in Constellations, we recognize that we often hold onto unconscious energy—thoughts that came from others and became our beliefs, or energy handed down to us in our very cells that affect our everyday lives. You have to be conscious of these thoughts in order to have an effect on them.

You would like to think you could affect that change consciously, but you cannot change an unconscious behavior strictly via conscious attention. To change an unconscious behavior, you first need to shift or release the energy stuck within the unconscious mind causing the behavior.

Dr. Bruce H. Lipton, a well-known expert in Quantum Physics and epigenetics who performed groundbreaking research at Stanford University's School of Medicine explains, "Both quantum physics and the new biology emphasize the influence of the mind's energy field. Consciousness is fundamental in shaping our life experiences."

"Conventional science and conventional allopathic medicine employ the idea that the body is a physical mechanism and can only respond to physical signals, hence the use of pharmaceuticals and drugs. However, there is a new understanding that completely changes our belief system because quantum physics reveals that energy is really the source of everything and so looking at the body as a physical entity is actually an illusion and incorrect understanding." *~Inner Evolution*, Bruce Lipton

Constellations "flip the switch," by getting to the energetic root of the unconscious thoughts by revealing the unconscious stories and trauma while releasing the energy causing the blocks or behaviors in the body. After the release, the movement of the soul begins the healing process in the unconscious and you find yourself engaging in positive behaviors without it even being a conscious change. It happens organically.

In other words, you do not have to think about the bad habit anymore; the new and healthier habits now take precedence. For example, a person who struggled with monogamy now finds joy in one partner. A person who has anxieties can live a normal life. A person who always feels abandoned soon finds themselves feeling loved and giving more love. **And it's not that you forget your past behavior; instead, the past no longer rules your present. And here's the beauty of it: the past will no longer dictate your future. You simply manifest a completely different, healthier, more robust and vibrant life.**

Family Constellation is a confidential work that uses the ancestral energetic connection that we all have to reveal unresolved traumas in the lives of previous family members and current generations. In one room, participants reconstruct their "family system" to identify and solve fundamental issues. They can choose to be observers, to represent a person in someone's else's family, or as a Seeker placing their family in the circle using Representatives. Family members are not required in the workshop. We each carry a "Knowing Field" (knowledge coming from the circle) that brings forth the phenomenon of "family presence" in the workshop.

A group workshop is led by a trained and certified facilitator. I prepare the room and hold space for truth, love and light to replace the blame, shame and guilt that we as humans inherently hold on to. Healing happens because we set a strong intention and take action by showing up for our family systems to be healed. After the truth is acknowledged, then I assist the Representatives in the healing process, setting strong energetic boundaries to create a healthy family system. **The result is family patterns are cleared out of the DNA strand that was causing the disruption of love and serenity all the way to the core issue.**

To participate in a healing Constellation, there is no need for formal training. Instead, these are learned abilities, where your intuition takes over, because you are tapping into the energy field of the seeker.

It is our responsibility on this planet to heal ourselves. As we are not here alone, it is our responsibility to help heal our families without continuing to become enmeshed and embroiled in unconscious patterns. It is possible to do this work and participate in powerful healing for your entire family.

Many people who witness Constellations for the first time often question if the Representatives are making all the information up. That is, until they themselves become a Representative. They soon experience the magic of the

"Knowing Field" in the circle of truth for themselves as they show up in that truth, and don't have reason to question it again.

Facilitators will begin a Family Constellation with an inquiring person: he or she will have a question or are likely dealing with a dilemma—a pattern of negative behavior or self-sabotage. Sometimes they simply have unearthed emotions that are confusing to them. This person is called The Seeker. The facilitators may then have Seekers pick a Representative and tell them who they are representing in their inquiry—generally themselves or a relative or friend connected to their lives that they are asking the Representative to represent, in that space of inquiry in the Constellation circle.

As popular as it is, this is not my style. I find the Constellations go deeper and faster when a Representative doesn't know who they are representing or the story of The Seeker. When they don't know, they are open to all truth other than what The Seeker may even know. It is truly powerful.

In this book, I have chosen to share case studies with you so that you might learn more quickly what type of work is brought effectively into the circle, and the powerful resolution that can come from it. In all the case studies I share with you in this book, blind representations (not knowing who they are representing or the story behind the representation), are always the case. In fact, most of the time the group in the circle has never met The Seeker until the day of the Constellation. Therefore, they have no idea who he or she is or what question The Seeker is asking.

There is most often an immediate transformation, and a very, very powerful beginning that takes place, with ongoing ripples of positivity for the next twelve to twenty-four months. Think about it: it took dozens of years, if not centuries, to sculpt your DNA and epigenetically pass on energy that doesn't serve. How wonderful, then, to immediately shift the overall energy in a positive way — and beautiful to experience ongoing, long-term transformation that is equally miraculous.

I invite you to read the case studies throughout the book. Place yourself in the position of The Seeker and allow yourself to resonate not only with the issues and stories brought up in the circle of truth, but the *overcoming* of them.

Your time is now. Give yourself permission to believe it's possible.

CHAPTER TEN

Signs That Patterns Might Be Running Your Life?

When I first started with Constellations, I had no idea how much trauma I had held in my body, and what systemic patterns, particularly fear, were running my life. As I began to see the release of patterns. My family started seeing changes in me and I shared what I was doing. Some wanted to explore the possibilities.

One day I was sitting in the circle, watching my son's Constellation as he was working on the ancestral line of his mother (me). A series of events came up in the circle that reflected my broken relationship with my own mother.

To my dismay, I witnessed how much of that brokenness between mother and grandmother that my son took on in his own body and his health. Feeling amazed at what was unfolding, I was able to clearly see something about myself that I had never understood before. It was life-changing, because I was able to comprehend so many aspects of my own unconscious secrets that were hidden, as a result of my experiences as a child.

Suddenly, the dysfunctional dynamics between mother and grandmother popped up. As the mother was instructed to speak the truth, the emotional impact of never feeling a mother's love caused an immediate release of trauma and stuck emotions. I even felt a huge wave of energy in my chest as their interaction began. Glancing up at my Representative,

I noticed her entire body was bright red. She began to tremble, and the surrounding Representatives immediately held her up to keep her from sinking into the ground. The facilitator checked on the Representative, who was fine, but at that very moment, Spirit whispered to me, "You have never fully entered your body!"

The truth shook me to the core. Something was unraveling within me.

I became completely coherent on every side of the entire experience that I was witnessing. Even though this had been my son's Constellation, I immediately felt the physical effects of shifting the DNA. Slowly, everything in my life began unfolding from an unconscious state to a more coherent state of Being.

The biggest impact of not entering my body, was realizing the lack of authenticity I had within my being to express myself, and to honor my higher self, rather than hide in unconscious fear. In doing that, I was beginning to awaken to how the mirror of that was reflecting all around me in my life, and I was able to see the impact this had on other people, especially my children, who were carrying some of the burden that showed up in their own relationships. I realized that my belief was that I had to work hard for love and money, because I did not deserve it, therefore I had to earn it. I could see what I was trying to fix in my children is the pattern I had passed on. I was able to recognize the inauthentic interactions I'd had trying to fix other relationships in my life, instead of me. Now that I could see myself, I could see others more clearly—their fullness and their experience without being in their business. I could be in a place of observing and supporting, instead of collapsing boundaries.

Immediately, my daughter, who had a lot of similar anxieties, began to feel like she could trust me, because now I could be listening and supportive. She began opening up more to me because I was listening through her eyes. She shared with me how much that I had changed and how much she enjoyed spending time with me. I loved it when she began calling me often, wanting to share her day and her life. I was amazed when all of my kids began opening up. Where I had guilt and shame just for being me before, so I felt compelled to fix, explain, defend myself or justify. But now I could listen and honor them, and they all felt it. I didn't have to be involved in their stuff. I could just love them.

In addition, my youngest son was able to share a hurtful situation in his youth with me that I hadn't known, where he had felt abandoned and rejected. He'd only been able to express this abandonment with outbursts of anger, which increased my guilt and defensiveness.

This time, however, I was able to listen to his anger without judgment, and without shame or defensiveness, and together we were able to pull down a barrier that had been there for decades.

"I realize that I haven't been a very good mother to you," I said. "I haven't been there for you. I was so caught up in my own stuff that I wasn't there for you. The impact on you was that you felt unloved by me."

"Mom I just needed you to hear the impact that it had on me. I know now you did the best you could. You're there for me now, and that's what matters." Then he gave me a big hug.

This was huge for us, because he had lost both parents in his own way as a young boy and had child attachment syndrome. Growing up without a father since age three exacerbated his feelings. He didn't have memories of me caressing him or holding him that he craved, even though that had happened frequently. I had nursed him until he was three, but unconsciously he had shut all that out.

At that moment we were able to bond, and he realized how much I loved him. My heart, which had been fully opened, was able to express all the love I have for him. I was finally able to see the experience through his eyes – the abandoned little boy grown up to be a man who hadn't been able to express deep hurts and pain. **This was monumental for him and for me and for our relationship.**

A series of events took place after that, leading me to many different healing experiences after this Constellation because the work had been done on the energetic level. It was a remarkably interesting experience when I learned how to fully enter my body. What followed was a compelling series of events that led to a path of discovery and connection with my own body and unconditional love for my Self.

CHAPTER ELEVEN

Our Body is a Walking History Book

Everyone enters this life through a family system. It is the biological, energetic connection of our ancestors--our DNA/blood related family system through whom we chose to enter into this three-dimensional life. Happily, or not, we all have one biological father and mother. They, in turn, have the same, giving you four biological grandparents, and so on.

Our free will began before we were even born. Spirit will never, ever take away our choice—before, during, or after life. In a profoundly moving children's book (also profoundly moving for adults) entitled, *The Little Soul in the Sun* by Neale Donald Walsh, the author clearly describes a process that we go through before we come to the planet. In the "Knowing Field" that I described earlier, we are able to discover more about our journey in life and why we chose our parentage in pre-life.

Before we came, we also chose siblings, friends, lovers, partners, and teachers. It is as if we are in a play, and we choose actors to enact our script. They agreed to act out a part to teach us what we decided we wanted to come to learn. That is the whole purpose of why our spirits are here: to gain knowledge and growth from our experiences.

It may seem difficult to imagine – especially if you have experienced extreme trauma - that you chose the players that would give you those experiences to learn from. From the trauma I experienced, I look back on it now and realize all my gifts, my strengths, and my paths in life were sculpted by what I suffered as a child, teen, and young adult.

Our body is a walking history book. Unexpressed pain and trauma are held in our bodies. We are finally at a time when the release of this is possible. We can shine the light upon our shadows. However, how can we do this if we are completely ignorant to the fact that we have shadows? Seek and you will find the answer in the circle as a seeker. Embracing our shadow is our journey to our Divine. This is an opportunity to do something big enough to reveal our blind spots and bring light to the shadows. Otherwise, we would go through life unaware that this is a story, an illusion, and a part of a much larger picture of evolutionary learning.

When we understand this, we allow a deeper awareness of our heart. Many past and current healers and philosophers are grounded in this understanding. As far back as Plato in the *Allegory of the Cave*, this master taught there was a difference between fixed realities and those we only *think* are real. He asked his students to imagine several slaves inside of a dark cavern who were facing one wall with a large fire behind them. The fire gave both heat and light to the cave, but the slaves spent their entire lives facing the wall, chained in only that one direction. All they could see were the shadows--it was literally all they knew. That was their reality, and they were content with their reality.

As you can imagine, they were only able to see the shadows of things instead of the real things themselves. For this reason, they gave *names* to the shadows. The slave didn't know that if he suddenly turned around, he would see three-dimensional objects and the beautiful colors of the fire, or the bright sun outside the cave. For a moment, that slave would be frightened by what he saw, and would want to return to what he'd only ever known and understood. But if it was possible for him to turn around for some time, then he could see the shadows weren't reality, and he might get excited by what he saw – and become more enlightened and conscious because of it. His ability to grow and expand would become much greater.

Imagine coming out from all you've ever known and seeing the sun – the ultimate truth of all things. Most people are unable to handle it all at once. The enormousness of the whole world frightens many, and some to death. The path is to move from shadows to firelight, and from firelight slowly to the sunlight. This is progressive learning, and Plato believed teachers are those who awaken others a bit at a time, to invite and allow this progression. However, sometimes we are not able to accept it, especially if we are still in our dark cave, avoiding the firelight and naming and blaming our shadows.

As long as we feel like life is "coming at us," we only feel like we are constantly combatting and reacting to life. Therefore, we will remain a *victim* to life. When we, however, recognize that this entire beautiful world of ours is our creation, then we are no longer a victim to circumstances. We will no longer feel small and powerless. We will see the challenges and obstacles for what they are – situations from which we can grow far stronger. And we will also be less afraid to tackle our shadows and what holds us back.

CHAPTER TWELVE

Personal or Systemic: What Does Systemic Even Mean?

When issues arise in your life, the facilitator can ask the Knowing Field if the issue is systemic or personal. It always reveals the answer. **Systemic** means you have inherited the vibrational pattern of one of your parent's family systems. **Personal** means you have developed a story or a pattern yourself, from something that has happened in your lifetime either as a child, teen, or young adult.

Every person is susceptible to this because we learn from the people around us. It can be as simple as a lifetime of witnessing your own parents' relationship. You may have unconsciously taken on their version of a relationship early as a child, and therefore you unconsciously attract similar issues in your own relationships. Again, this is a story you saw and then constructed, so it is personal.

Many times, the answer comes up as *both* systemic and personal because your systemic pattern has a vibration that may have caused you to attract similar circumstances in your life. It becomes a personal issue as well, because it had a deeply profound impact on your life and the story you are holding onto.

We all have a God-given right to belong to our family system we were born in. It is what it is, and nothing can change that. In addition, when you are cut out of your own biological system because of circumstances, behaviors, divorce, death, or adoption, and you are not acknowledged in your proper place in that family system, then a disruption may occur that often will affect others in your family system as well as you.

This disruption can cause an energetic repercussion, because love and connection have been lost in some form or another. This is a common occurrence in the situation of divorce or adoption. We call it a *systemic issue* in your family system. Whether big or small, every spirit in the family system is crying out to be acknowledged. If you have been cut off, you are yearning to be acknowledged for your time on this earth. So are each of your familial connections.

More critical than someone cutting you off from your own family system is when you cut yourself off from one or both of your parents due to whatever pain or judgments you may have toward them. You do not necessarily have to invite them into your life, especially not, for example, your dad sexually abused you and your mother went along with it. Yet energetically, there is another story. You chose to come through that family system for a reason. You are who you are because of that choice.

Now, if you cut your parents off without going to the core of the issue energetically, you cut yourself off from your family system. You then risk falling into the category of Spiritual bypassing, because you are denying the truth of the shadow or soul wound that exists between you and your parents. This can be especially true if you do energy or healing work. Spiritual bypassing indicates you have a shadow that you are overriding, suppressing, avoiding, or distracting by seeking the light to overcome it, rather than going to the depth that it will require to resolve the issue. Spiritual bypassing is when you cut yourself off from your own deeper truth.

Since our God Source never violates our free will, nothing is forced upon you. Energetically and vibrationally, you carry a piece of your family system in you in some form or another. It could be the very issue that is causing your trigger with one or more parents. If you are in judgment of your parents about something, it often implies that you are mirroring or carrying the vibration of that same issue in your own DNA. Therefore, you may unconsciously be passing it on in your family system.

Patterns are real. You may continue to see these pop up in your relationships and in your children and their relationships if you continue to resist addressing that part of you. Or you may be continually attracting that same issue or circumstance with someone outside of your family system. I see that all the time with clients that I work with. I had to learn to see it in myself, even though I resisted it for many years. Eventually the pattern showed itself too strongly for me to ignore. I had to acknowledge that I was abused as a child by my angry father, and I inherited my mother's suppressed rage.

Because of this, I married an abusive man with a lot of anger, and it added to the suppressed rage I already carried inside of me from my mother's lifetime, and mine. It would take acknowledging it and doing the work in order to clear the pattern and the DNA.

CHAPTER THIRTEEN

Big Souls Make Big Promises

As I shared earlier, I was spiritual bypassing before I uncovered a suppressed rage. It was completely unconscious and contained until it was not. My mother would not allow herself to experience emotions, so she would turn her babies over to my dad for harsh abuse for crying, rather than administering a mother's loving discipline. She confined her babies to a crib for having any emotion. I had shut out my entire childhood. It did not exist.

Because of this work, I was able to discover and own the triggers that would cause reactions to things because I could not see or acknowledge that pattern of suppressed rage. As a seeker in the circle, I had the courage to see it for what it was and finally address it head on. It brought in tremendous blessings to my family, as I was able to clean up these patterns in my own life and help my adult children do the same. I was also able to bring light to that blind spot as a healer, becoming a more powerful, clear-seeing facilitator.

When you have done the deeper work yourself, you can empathically feel inauthentic behavior when someone is spiritual bypassing. For example, they may seem overly spiritual, humble, confident, or happy *all* of the time. This may feel attractive to those seeking happiness who are dealing with similar issues, but because the behaviors are contrived, eventually it will feel inauthentic and difficult to fully connect on a deeper level unless you are in a similar pattern. While outwardly seeming savvy on spiritual matters, they easily trigger deeper issues and many times project on others.

Healer or not, to be clear, no one can fully access their deeper truth and bring light to their shadow side if they have cut themselves off from their own family system. The more judgment you have on your parents, the more indication that you are subconsciously mirroring that vibration in your energy field.

I discovered that we all have a shadow side, and if we override it or ignore it then it may sneak up on us and...boom! Continual self-sabotage knocks at our door until the shadow of our ancestors is acknowledged and dealt with and our family system is intact. I unconsciously thought I was broken because of my abuse, so I became a healer trying to fix everyone because I was spiritually bypassing. I was constantly trying to fix everyone else, including my children.

There is another important truth that showed up as a glaring reality on my own healing path and personal experience. Whatever I withheld or whomever I shut out or resisted in my own family system was most often what I either created in that very pattern of my personal life or I passed it onto my children to deal with. In other words, my children's biggest systemic issues were coming from my side of the family system, myself, and my shutdown mother.

What a shock! I was the calm one of the family rather than their father, who was a raging mad man at times. Therefore, I had to face the cruel fact that by withholding and suppressing my unconscious emotions as an infant, I was more apt to pass issues onto my children as well as project onto my participants.

Because I was unconscious of my own suppressed rage, I passed it on to several of my children. My husband's rage was open, so I assumed my children had inherited their issues from their dad. But when my daughter had the facilitator test her issue, it did not come from her dad's side. It came from her mother's and the Representative for her mother began berating men in the circle because of the suppressed rage toward her father that had never been expressed. After the healing took place and the Constellation was complete, my daughter sat there, stunned. She said, "Mom, everything your Representative said to the men I have said to my husband, word-for-word."

I finally witnessed in a Constellation what my mom experienced as a child, and I heard the very words that had defined my entire life: "I can't stop the abuse!". I suddenly realized I had been living *her* life, attracting a man that was emotionally abusive. I did not recognize it as abuse because I had been abused, yet I was torn up inside my entire life because I could not stop his rage and disrespect toward me in front of my children.

At first, after hearing those words, I was furious at my mother for not dealing with her own stuff and leaving it for me to deal with. Afterward, I spent a good twenty-four hours embracing the shame of it all until it left my body for good. I soon realized what a gift it was to be able to do my mom's healing work. It was at that profound moment I thought "big souls make big promises."

That is why I love Constellations. The seeker and I just sit in a chair and watch as if a movie were playing out. I don't have to fix anything; the circle does it for them, and they see what they see. They witness it for themselves and there is no bypassing the truth of the circle unless you choose to deny it as truth, and that is a choice as well.

Now I can talk about my past without all the guilt and shame that was in my body that belonged to my mother. I was able to clear her passed on emotions and my own. That is why I am here today as a Constellation facilitator. My gifts as a facilitator are what they are because of my childhood experiences, not in *spite* of them.

I am a gift to the circle because I have faced my demons and my dark side. I am dedicated and devoted to the service of others experiencing the same freedom as I am experiencing at this very moment. There is no more self-sabotage, and I am free of blame, shame, and guilt, and am able to more fully love my children because I fully and deeply love all of me.

The same is true for you. Conscious or unconscious, whatever you withhold or suppress, your children will be next in line to have to deal with it. I had been completely unconscious of it. That's why I'm sharing with you. The more conscious you are, the more you can heal. The less your children must deal with ancestral trauma, the more they are free to live a happy, healthy, beautiful life. And your grandchildren? Believe me, they will be that much healthier and happier, too.

CHAPTER FOURTEEN

Your Soul Knows When It Is Time

Family Constellations can seem a difficult concept to grasp at first, but the truth of it will plant itself as a little seed inside of you and it will grow if you allow it to. Why is this important? If you are continually struggling to heal mental, physical, and emotional issues in your life, but can never seem to get on the other side of them and live a productive life, you likely have deeper healing to do. Just as we all have ancestors, we all have layers of ancestral DNA and triggers.

For example, you may think you have "forgiven" your parents, but there is a residual judgment because you have not witnessed the truth from your parents' points of view or circumstances. Without that, you cannot truly experience the gratitude for what your parents went through to give you the rights and full membership into your family system.

No matter what your parents have done, it is not your job to put them in a place of judgment. Until you take the opportunity to fully witness life from their eyes, including the burdens they were carrying, you are not in a position to judge them.

The opposite can also occur. If you have held your parents on a pedestal where they can do no wrong, it means you may be tied to your parents in an unhealthy way. I want to caution you that you might be trying to measure up to the projection of your perfect parent. You may be trying to live an identity that isn't your truth. *All parents* have a shadow side. Your parents may be trying to get you to live their path, but their path is not yours. This is a common tragedy I see often. By not living your own life, it fractures the soul and affects everyone around you. Your parents may also be bypassing and better at hiding it from their children than others, and this too can be an ancestral trait.

The incredibly good news is that either side of this pendulum, whether judgment or perfection projection can be dealt with in the circle, too. When we say, "I take back what is mine, and give you what is yours," you are helping to cut and clear identities so that you and all in your ancestral and descendent lines may be your authentic selves. You can more fully claim your true and authentic identity.

BEYOND TRAUMA:
HONEST HEALING, PROFOUND TRANSFORMATION

There is a beautiful young girl, very dear to me, who comes at least once a year to do a Constellation. She used to be bi-polar/manic depressive, with panic attacks and high anxiety. She rarely left her house because she was over-stimulated by crowds. She had no energy most of the time and was unable to keep up her house to her standards, which was also depressing her. When I tested her, the hot issue almost always pointed to systemic issues.

After a few Constellations, she confided in me that each time she looked back on the Constellations a year later, she realized just how drastically her life had changed because of it. That's why she has made Constellations a priority of her inner work and her ongoing life.

Four years later, she no longer has episodes of any sort. Instead, she is working fulltime and attending college. Her house is always organized -- the opposite of how it used to look. She told me her life is not perfect, but she's delighted she took her life back by getting ancestral shadows out of her energy field--the only part of her life she could control. Now that she is no longer living the life of her ancestors, she is free to live her own, and that freedom means the world to her.

Some people want it all fixed in one session. "When am I going to live my life?" they cry.

I explain that after completing all four grandparents, they will feel the freedom of the past and be ready to work on their own personal issues. Many people will do the work for one grandparent and want immediate results. I tell them, "It took hundreds of years to develop these issues, so be patient in taking at least a few Constellations to work out all four sets of grandparents' issues." Be patient and be willing to do the work. The strength of your intention and your willingness to be open and to believe in your role as a seeker in the circle will determine the time it may take.

Here's a clue to some puzzling patterns you may be seeing in your relationships, or those of your parents and your children. The following systemic patterns usually show up as chronic patterns with money, love issues, or illnesses that interrupt your life or relationships:

- Betrayal
- Infidelity
- Emotional shut down
- Self-Sabotage
- Depression
- Anxieties
- Addictions
- Extreme introverted behaviors
- Reoccurring dialogue
- Obsessive/compulsive behaviors
- Passiveness/aggressive behaviors

- Seemingly unresolvable conflicts
- Possessiveness
- Anger/rage
- Unresolved fears
- Limitations
- Scarcity mindset
- Body issues/extreme vanity
- Eating disorders
- Infertility
- Chronic illnesses
- Trauma/stress
- Excessive fears

Facilitators of Family Constellations won't claim to cure illness. Still, every experience in this life is fueled by energy and vibration. By clearing out the negative energy lodged within the matrix system that stops the flow of energy, you are giving your body a free flow of renewed energy and higher vibration to bring a powerful new life force to sustain a healthy balance that supports freedom of choice.

The following are examples of personal issues that have been put into the circle during Family Constellation:

- Abundance block/find out where your blocks for money lie
- Parent/inner child/self-love and compassion
- Balance of male and female energy
- Accessing, receiving and becoming one with Divine Feminine/Masculine
- Discovering your issues that are ancestral
- Relationships/resolve conflicts/who is available/is it sustainable

- Unresolved deaths/miscarries/abortions
- Chronic Illnesses
- Back pain/shoulder/knees/hips/neck, etc.
- Excessive behavioral problems with your child
- Why your baby keeps fussing or crying
- Finding your purpose
- Setting up your business plan
- Marketing plan/branding
- Employee honesty or work ethics
- Family dynamics/patterns that cause conflict
- Divorce mediation or issues children take on from divorce
- Behavior problems with your pets
- Business consultation to learn more about your demographics
- Investments
- Curses removed
- Boundaries work
- Parent/child boundaries

I have witnessed so many beautiful, life-changing miracles that have happened in the circle. Therefore I'm very passionate about giving others this opportunity to see the magic for themselves. You can experience the benefits of healing the disruptive DNA and creating more transformative wellness. It is not necessary to continue struggling from mental, emotional, spiritual, physical, and financial stress and trauma that could be changed so easily and inexpensively. I invite you to see for yourself. Not only am I living my dream and an extraordinary life, I know that you can, too.

CHAPTER FIFTEEN

Case Studies

REPLACING THE HAMSTER WHEEL:
WHOSE LIFE WAS I LIVING? WHAT AGREEMENTS DID I MAKE?

In this book, we have compiled case studies so you can see the journeys of other individuals, in what transformations they have been able to create in great moments of insight and conscious awareness to help them take a deep dive into their healing and their family's healing. These involve sensitive issues. The subjects have given me permission to share their stories. In certain situations, names have been changed to protect their privacy, but other information has remained the same so you can benefit from their healing.

CASE STUDY #1
I WAS CONCERNED ABOUT MY DAUGHTER. I DIDN'T KNOW THAT
I WAS PROJECTING ANCESTRAL DISTRUST TOWARD WOMEN

Family History: Janet was genuinely concerned with her daughter's behavior. She was approaching fifteen years old and growing apart from her three brothers. Also, lately she seemed so put off by her mother. Janet was from a very traditional and rigid patriarchal family. Her grandfather from her dad's side was very bitter toward women because his own wife had left him. Janet's mom eventually left Janet's dad as well, and he carried on the bitterness toward women. Janet's dad turned to Janet when she was younger to vent about his divorce with her mom. Now, as a grown mother, she avoided him and his bitterness toward her mother and women in general. Janet also felt like her husband did not respect her as well.

The Circle Revealed: At a young age, Janet took on her father's and grandfather's judgment on the female species, considering them weak and untrustworthy. The bitterness was unconsciously affecting her own ability to love and connect with her own Divine and her daughter. Janet was unconsciously carrying her dad's negative energy toward women in general and it drastically spilled over to her daughter. Janet's Representative was overtaken and had to lie down when she began opening her heart to Divine love and connection to the feminine energy that she had been unconsciously denying herself.

Resolution: Janet discovered she was projecting and had shut down her own heart to love and connection from ancestral bitterness. She knew she felt responsible for her dad's misery after divorce, so she had avoided him, but did not know how to stop taking that on emotionally. Boundaries were set, and she was able to heal the disconnect with her daughter after she realized she had a pattern of treating her daughter as if she were less than the boys in the family.

Comments: Most often, we are projecting on others whatever our body is carrying because it is buried in our unconscious state. In many circumstances, children are loyal and play out their parents' unresolved issues in their own marriage because they have unconsciously taken on the problems—and because that is all they know. They experience conflict with themselves and create it outside of themselves. In Janet's case, this was definitely an ancestral pattern, and Janet was able to break the cycle. She later told us that the best part was how she shifted everything in her relationship with her daughter, and greatly improved her relationship with her husband.

Case Study #2
I Was Miserable in Relationships and Struggled with a Compulsion Toward Infidelity

Joseph was nearly full-blood Lakota, although he had some French ancestry. and his native mother carried a French name. He could drink more than most without becoming inebriated. In addition, Joseph carried a lot of shame and guilt from having affairs during a marriage that eventually failed. He entered another relationship that also ended in affairs. Joseph expressed that he did not know why he could not stop cheating during his marriages. He was not happy because he felt so much shame and self-loathing. He expressed deep disgust regarding himself and his behaviors. He could not admit, however, that he was an alcoholic until he did a ceremony where he had to face his demons.

Family History: Joseph's great-great-grandfather was a French trapper. His great-great-grandmother was Lakota. She had a son by him and raised him within the tribal community. Her son then married a native woman and had a son that carried on the French name. This son was taken from his mother at a young age and raised in the mandated Native American boarding schools run by Caucasian administrators and teachers, where not only his culture was taken from him, but also his innocence as he experienced sexual abuse.

Joseph's grandfather then married and carried that sexual abuse in to his family, sexually abusing his daughter who eventually became Joseph's mom. Because of her own abuse, Joseph's mother struggled in her relationship with Joseph's father.

The Circle Revealed: Joseph's great-great-grandfather, the French trapper, showed signs of being inebriated and incoherent. His great-great-grandmother's Representative in the circle expressed she had been raped by him, which resulted in a son that was considered half-breed at the time. Both parents of the child expressed deep inner shame toward the child because of the circumstances of the conception. Her son's Representative said he felt like he was split down the middle, a result of his parents' conflicting cultures and the shame of his circumstances. The Representative expressed an extreme amount of shame in his body. When the so-called "half breed" son then had a son of his own, his son in turn was very angry with his father who had treated him poorly because of his own self-hatred and personal struggles. All of these trickles of sexual abuse and shame led to Joseph's seemingly uncontrollable urges to drink and sleep with women outside of his relationships.

Resolution: The relationship between Joseph's great-great-grandparents was healed. Both parents acknowledged and embraced the shame they carried and apologized to their son. Their son's relationship with his own child was addressed and healed. Joseph could see clearly that he had been living his great-great-grandfather's life—a man who spent his adulthood drinking to cover up the shame of his sexual behaviors. Joseph was very relieved to see that the shame was not his to carry, and happy to witness their healing process take place. He said afterward that he felt so much lighter and free to live his own life, forgive his own behaviors, and move on without his paralyzing addictions.

Comments: As you can see, the behavior in Joseph's life could be traced back and connected to the actions of his great-great-grandfather. Love and connection were restored, while the burden was lifted from Joseph so he, in turn, could live his own life fully. The circumstances and struggles in Joseph's life were a direct result of his great-great-grandfather's actions.

What shows up in the circle when you are The Seeker is what you have been carrying, and many times, the life you are living. Severe trauma and shame where love and connection are lost passes down from generation to generation. Joseph had no idea that he was acting out the shame from four generations back. It is very common to carry four generations of trauma that continues to manifest itself by attracting similar circumstances in generations to come. Through Constellations, it is possible to break cycles, release compulsions and addictions, and release ancestral trauma from the body.

All it takes is one day of sitting in the circle and either watching the magic happening or participate as a Representative and you know that you have tapped into the energy field as a representation of the witnessing that takes place. The real magic is the Representatives always get chosen for a part they needed to process their own issues. Without even sitting in the Seeker chair, they walk away feeling the movement and cleansing of the soul.

I love this work because it clearly changes lives and leaves everyone in the community connected at a soul level. It is a beautiful and satisfying reward that words cannot even describe. Even for those that do not want their business exposed to the rest, there is no pressure to reveal the identity of those representing. You can choose to keep your Constellation confidential because no one knows who they are representing.

CHAPTER SIXTEEN

Preparing for Family Constellation Workshops

The purpose of this section is to empower you to gather the information that may be helpful in having a Family Constellation done successfully—with the greatest impact for you and your family system. We have found that in the act of having gathered this information, you have already begun a movement, in what Bert Hellinger calls 'the soul of the family"* – a systemic movement. The knowledge you gather energetically and intellectually allows great movement. In some cases, if not enough information is present about family, a facilitator may even have to stop a Constellation.

Begin this process, allowing yourself to gather one step at a time. If you feel overwhelmed, just pick what is important to you and come back to the rest later.

Your family system includes:

- **Your nuclear family.** This includes you and your spouse and children. It is impacted at times by the history of former partners (marital partners or lovers) of either or both of the spouses, and children who are born outside of that relationship, as well as children who died, were miscarried, or aborted.

- **Your family of origin.** This includes you and your siblings, your parents and their siblings, and their parents.

It sometimes includes your great grandparents and the former spouses or lovers of parents or grandparents.

- **Your extended family.** In communities which have a rich history of active extended family, there may be greater prevalence of Constellations that include cousins, and Constellations which reveal traumas further back in the ancestral line. These can continue to impact those living today.

You may use the following in discovering what traumas may have impacted your family system. If any of these incidents occurred, they might be important and have wide-reaching effects within your family system. It is also apparent that a specific trauma may not impact you or your immediate system. If you choose not to reveal these issues, let the facilitator know that you are choosing to withhold certain information. It is all about choice, there is no right or wrong way, there is no judgment in the circle.

- Did anyone die young -- i.e. before reaching adulthood?
- Were there any suicides in the family?
- Were there any parents who died before their children were adults?
- Were there any abortions or miscarriages? If so, find out in which trimester it occurred.
- Was anyone seriously ill for a significant portion of his or her life? Include mental illness.
- Was anyone disowned or disinherited by their family--i.e. cast out?
- Was anyone denied his or her inheritance?
- Were there deep issues of class or culture conflicts in marriages?
- Did anyone have a serious birth defect?
- Were there any stillborn children?

- Was there any physical abuse, sexual abuse, or rape anywhere in the family?

- Were there any children given away at birth?

- Were any children adopted?

- Were there any alcoholics or drug addicts?

- Was anyone in your family system murdered?

- Did anyone commit any criminal actions or go to jail for anything? Were they held as a prisoner of war?

In addition, did either of your parents have significant relationships prior to marrying? This is particularly important if they were engaged. If so, find out who broke off the relationship and if there were any hard feelings held by either person afterward.

You will want to research whether there might be any victims that were exploited by your family and ancestors. For example, if your great-grandparents were slave owners, those who were brutalized or victimized by your ancestors may be connected to your family system awaiting acknowledgment. Another situation might be one in which your ancestors owned a large corporation. For example, let's consider that your grandfather owned a mining company. There might be victims connected to your system if there had been a mining tragedy where someone was either killed or seriously wounded. The particulars of the incident might never have been known to anyone outside the upper level of management. It might have been that the owner did not allow for proper bracing or did not adhere to the safety measures because they would have cut into profits.

In looking for the story in your family system, you may simply want to reflect. You may want to speak with relatives, but hopefully with respect and reserve when issues are difficult for others to speak of. You may want to see what is available in your family records. Part of the work is beginning to see.

The title of one of Bert Hellinger's books is telling: *Acknowledging What Is"* When we gently move away from what Hunter Beaumont sometimes calls "family propaganda", we come to the space where we honor that everyone in a family system has the right to belong.

It is helpful if the facilitator has information regarding specifics, but it is not always necessary. This work is without judgment. We look at the truth of what has impacted or injured the family system, and then a movement begins in the system that seems to quiet the resonance of the trauma: grace.

I have witnessed a family whose great-grandfather committed murder, against his siblings and other families. Untimely deaths continue to occur annually to this day within that family system because the victims have no resolve nor the one committing the murder.

Ancestral gathering information was compiled with the help of Francesca Mason Boring

CHAPTER SEVENTEEN

Hidden Identities and Treasures of Truth Revealed

CASE STUDY #3
MEETING MY MOTHER FOR THE FIRST TIME

At birth, Susan was placed with an adoption agency who put her in foster care for six months until suitable parents could be found. She grew up fiercely independent, distrusting of adults in general, and having to be in control. Her adoptive parents were very good to her, educating her well and providing a loving home and family life. Still, she sometimes exhibited behaviors that were unhealthy. She was puzzled with her self-sabotage during much of her life, especially because it happened every spring. She married an abusive spouse and stayed with him for seventeen difficult years before leaving him to protect her children. Despite being smart and artistically talented, she continued to fight her self-sabotage — an unhealthy part of her that she couldn't explain.

FIRST CONSTELLATION

Family History: Susan knew virtually nothing about her biological relatives and avoided DNA tests because she didn't want to hurt anyone—especially her wonderful adoptive parents. Secretly, she longed to know her true history. An adopted child, even in wonderful adoptive circumstances, generally carries wounds of abandonment and questions why she or he was given up for adoption in the first place. Once her adoptive father passed away, however, he let her know she had his approval to find her birth parents. Resulting DNA matches found only distant cousins and was confusing, so she didn't pursue more information about the matches. She walked away from the confusion. It was too disturbing to continue without clarity, knowing that if she was still a secret, it could be disrupting to certain birth family members.

The Circle Revealed: During Susan's first Constellation, her intention was to access energy regarding her adoptive family and her self-sabotage, which it did and surprised her with how quickly it worked. The energy in the circle also revealed that her birth family wanted to be involved in a greater way. Susan went on to attend our four-day Constellation retreat coupled with equine therapy. Knowing virtually nothing about her birth family for five decades, suddenly as a result of the last Constellation, two days before the retreat she had discovered her connection to over fifty new direct family members by meeting her birth uncle for the first time. During the time spent with the horses at the retreat, Susan was able to recognize and let go of the cycle of her fierce, unhealthy independence in order to do the necessary work for her birth family. She went on to meet her birth mother, stepfather, and younger brothers. She has since enjoyed having a great relationship with both her biological parents and he adopted parents.

CHAPTER EIGHTEEN

The Nature of Emotional Reality

To know ourselves is to become aware of the true nature of our reality. We have some of the most powerful access to our true reality through Family Constellations. We are all connected to a family system, so now with greater knowledge we can transform negative patterns into conscious awareness. When we bring forth this brilliant white light of truth, it integrates right into the body of dense shadow energy that we hold (trauma, pain, anger, addiction, etc.). We are then able to transcend and transmute our own darkness into beautiful light. The truth really does set us free.

Anytime we participate in Family Constellations as a modality, we are transforming as beings for the betterment of *all beings*, great or small. We heal broken group consciousness by releasing the stories of our childhood and ancestral shame. Once we release our past stories, we are retrieving our innocence that was at one time lost in that story. Therefore, bringing back that child within us means we have the freedom to experience joy, love, and trust once again. It is powerful, beautiful, and can be miraculous.

There is a huge difference between forgiveness and "fixing" our relationships. Forgiveness lets go of the need to fix. It allows us to seek righteous indignation in our truths, and to live life without judgment or vengeance. Instead of the old patterns of so easily accessing blame, shame, and guilt while denying our inherent access to truth, love, and light, we shift the power dynamics back to personal responsibility. And rather than just survive, we can move forward with grace. We can unleash our power and our life purpose.

I met a beautiful woman at a gathering named Marin. She appeared to be very composed, yet she seemed to be covering up her true feelings. She was not really expressive of her emotion, even when happy—much less when she was scared or uncomfortable. Marin and I became friends, and she began confiding in me about her past relationships. I listened to her talk with empathy, and then I asked Marin if she realized she was a man-hater. She told me later, that question caused her to take a deeper look within, more than anything she had experienced before that moment.

We enjoyed our time together and I shared with her how Family Constellations could help access family patterns. After explaining the work I did, Marin immediately said she knew that was what she felt called to do in order to shift things in her life.

"I have lived a life of shame," she admitted. "I want something different now."

I believed the conviction I saw in her eyes. As the days progressed, Marin shared with me that she was raped twice at the age of seventeen. The first rape, she revealed, happened when she went on a blind date her friend had set up for her. It ended in horrific violence. His behavior was so bizarre and ruthless that she felt that her life was in danger. She did not dare scream, cry, say, or do anything to stop him.

After that, Marin was filled with fear about men, but tried to love again. The second rape occurred when she was sleeping outside with her new boyfriend. His brother woke her up with him on top of her. She was afraid the two other boys sleeping next to them would wake up and gang rape her, so she did not scream, cry, say, or do anything, once again. This seemed to be a pattern. She told no one of either incident and had done nothing to prosecute these men. I could feel the guilt, the horror, the shame, and the repressed anger, and the deep, deep sadness this violence had affected upon her now as an adult and a single mother of a little girl.

Soon after, Marin called to announce she was ready to do a Constellation on her rapes. She had talked with her mom about her rapes and her mother confessed she was raped seven times before she was fifteen. She, too, had told no one. Marin's maternal grandmother was not alive, so it was unknown to her at that time where the pattern started. I was traveling to Southern Utah to do a workshop there, so I invited her to come with me and participate. We stayed in a rental, and I was not surprised to learn after her experiences just how important it was for her to have her own room, as she was terrified of having others in the room while she slept.

When I set up her Constellation, I put a Representative for both men who had raped her. In addition, I added Representatives for Anger, Shame, the Feminine Divine with the Masculine Divine to support the process, and then, of course, made sure Marin was represented in the circle.

As Marin sat in the chair next to me, she watched her Representative express what was never expressed to these men. I kept a close eye on her because I was trained not to retraumatize victims of abuse. I expected her to show some emotion, but she was composed while observing the interactions going on in the circle. She was stable and aware, as she wanted to be sure everything was said that needed to be said. She was very clear about that.

As the circle progressed, I asked her if she wanted to go into the circle and face the two Representatives of her predators to get completion. She was more than willing, and courageously went into the circle and expressed everything she was never able to express. Still, the emotions were not present. I had faith; I knew everything had been dealt with on the energetic level and the physical healing would soon follow.

While it is different for everyone, it doesn't always take a week or a few months for the movement of the soul to bring healing to the surface of stored up emotions and trauma that needed to be released. For Marin, this happened soon after her session; she began to feel sick. She went to her bedroom and had to lie down. She wanted to be alone and began crying. The emotions that couldn't be released in the circle were being released behind the safety of closed doors for her. She was finally releasing the trauma, fear, anger, rage, and self-loathing that had been tucked away for close to twenty years.

I checked on her periodically and put on my playlist of healing music for her. She had released so much that she was exhausted. Still, she found it impossible to rest. I sat up through the night with her so she could feel safe. It was only in participating in this Constellation that she was able to look at her patterns clearly. She had attracted a lifetime of horrendous relationships with men. Now, however, instead of living in shame and guilt from that, she was able to quit blaming herself and see that she had been a victim in the rapes. She realized she had remained in that victim narrative with everything else that followed in her life because she had not dealt with those two incidents.

Her release of emotions from this travesty was nearly over by morning. She realized she was able to move on and raise her consciousness and her frequency so she could see her past relationships for what they were, period. Now, she could also have a true hope of a relationship with a man filled with respect and deeper meaning.

Curious, she took my Dynamics and Differences class where I teach about relationships, and Marin began to open her eyes to the side of a man she had never known before. She realized that while she had attracted the small percentage of disrespectful men in the world, there *were* men – even strangers – that looked out for her safety. Before this, there had only been one older man who had been kind and loving to her, but she had never allowed herself to be loved by him. She decided to allow him into her life in order to see an entirely new version of what men could be. It turned out to be a beautiful friendship, and Marin became a strong advocate for men.

Sexuality, sexual violence, and infidelity all cause a measure of deep shame in a human body and in the traits handed down from one generation to another.

CONSTELLATION CASE STUDY #4
MY GREAT-GRANDMOTHER DIED SHORTLY AFTER HER HUSBAND FORCED HER TO ABORT THEIR SECOND CHILD

Adrianne had an extensive history of sexual shame and hiding her gifts. She was told by many facilitators that she was hiding from herself.

"I have had a lot of guilt and shame for things in my past, and I keep getting told I am hiding. I don't know any other way to deal with life."

She had known of this trauma in her family history but had no idea how it had impacted her own life.

Family History: Adrienne's great-great-grandmother Evelyn became pregnant when she already had a two-year-old little girl. Her husband said they couldn't afford another child. Abortion was illegal, so he insisted that she allow him to abort the baby because it was not legal at the time, even though that went against all her morals.

Evelyn died a short time after. Her death certificate says she died from a forest fire, but the family believes she may have died from gangrene, due to the abortion. In that same ancestral line, there were two other forced abortions known to Adrianne, forced upon her grandmother and her aunt. Evelyn's granddaughter (Adrianne's mother) had experienced multiple sexual assaults because she did not realize she had unconsciously brought her grandmother's energy forward. Adrianne decided to break the cycle.

The Circle Revealed: Evelyn died in a state of horrible regret, trauma, and shame. She was so devastated she could not forgive herself. During the Constellation Evelyn's Representative kept trying to leave the circle to hide under tables, chairs, or whatever she could find to hide from her shame. She did not feel worthy of forgiveness; she was stuck in her own hell. She had unexpressed anger toward her husband for insisting on the abortion.

Resolution: Once she expressed all of her stored-up emotions toward her husband and her regret toward her unborn baby, Evelyn was able to reconcile with herself and find forgiveness for herself. Adreanne was then able to observe the feelings she was carrying on behalf of her great-great-grandmother and realize they did not belong to her.

Adreanne has now uncovered her gifts, recognizing freedom away from the shame, transcending into self-love. Her powerful body-intuitive gifts are now helping hundreds of others.

Comments: Emotions can be so traumatic that they continue as long as four generations, or more, creating unusual circumstances of shame, blame, and guilt in the lives of posterity. In this case, Adreanne was able to break this cycle for her mother, herself, and her daughter.

CHAPTER NINETEEN

The Nature of Physical Reality

I had been doing this work long enough to recognize that physical symptoms also have emotional origins. Then one day, it happened: my eyesight started deteriorating so badly that I could not see well, even with the strongest glasses. Diagnosed as having cataracts and corneal dystrophy, I knew it was ancestral because my mother had cataracts removed and a cornea transplant. Both of my grandfathers had gone blind and my oldest son was also diagnosed with the same eye disease.

I wanted to get some bodywork done for my eyes, so I went to a session with one of my participants who had been going to my Constellation workshops for a year. She had become a very gifted healer. As she placed her hands on my eyes, she asked, "Who's eyes are these?"

"They are my mom's and my grandpa's," I replied without thinking, only knowing.

This gifted healer said the energy from my eyes represented the distorted view of women in religion. That made sense to me because of how I had struggled with the belief that I had to submit to men, due to my upbringing in a fundamentalist Mormon religion that practiced polygamy and being beaten into submission.

"It's going to take a Constellation to release all the energy you have around your eyes, Shauna, because it is too much for my skills."

I quickly gathered a group and a facilitator for a Constellation to be done for my eyes and was grateful for the men and women who showed up. I was taught in my training that Mother Nature will often participate in Family Constellations because we are all connected to everything, including Mother Nature. Her energy has a place in the circle of truth. I have seen it many times in the past, but this incident I will never forget.

It was a beautifully sunny and warm day in July. During the circle of the Constellation, we brought in a Representative for my mother and a Representative for her distorted view of religion.

The facilitator was working to heal the distortion and then approached my mother's Representative. Suddenly, my mother's Representative was overcome with fear. "I don't want to see the truth!" she cried out.

At that very moment, lightning struck outside. Yet there had not been a cloud in the sky on this heated midsummer day.

"That was a sign that Mother Nature has joined our circle!" I exclaimed, feeling it to my very bones. Everyone else did, too. They didn't have a choice.

After that stunning show of appearance, the healing began for my mother's Representative and she eventually had a change of heart. It was quite a process. She was willing to take back her power that she had given to the patriarchal demands in her polygamist family and culture. Words of acknowledgment and forgiveness were spoken.

"I want to see now!" the Representative declared. Then. . .you guessed it: at that very moment, lightning struck again only this time it hit the building or close to it. We all jumped in unison as it shook the building to its very foundation—and turned on the alarm to the clubhouse all at once.

It was a profound moment for all of us to see the power and acknowledgment of Nature joining our circle. We were also very aware of the importance of healing this patriarchal misinterpretation of power. It was very powerful and succinct. The chaos that followed the alarm going caused us to convene the Constellation the next day. We all agreed and had a good laugh as we went on our way.

When we set up the Constellation the next day to complete the work on my mother for my eyes, the Representative for my mother was able to access and express the very words that defined my entire life, conscious and unconscious. "I can't stop the abuse," exactly what I had recently learned from my past about my abuse. It all made sense to me. It was word-for-word what I had been feeling since opening up my soul wounds around my dad. This also explained the guilt I carried for my husband's emotional abuse toward my children and myself with his rage. My mom had witnessed her little sister and herself being abused as a child. No one believed her because it was a family member, so she lived a life of shut down emotions and suppressed rage that I took on in her womb.

I was living *her* life. I was carrying on her trauma from her childhood that she had never talked about, and she had completely shut down her emotions and submitted to my dad rather than live her truth. She had been through so much in her life and had never had a chance to heal. My grandfather's stories came up in a Constellation for him as well.

My mother had bad eyes. She did not want to see too much of the pain of her own life. I was incredibly grateful, then, to be able to heal my mother's trauma, and therefore release the negative energy surrounding my own eyes. Our bodies are made of natural elements and connected to nature.

It was an experience I will never forget. Our bodies are the greatest representation of nature. In fact, we are over 80% water, which is known to be malleable and carry precise information. Most chronic illnesses are caused by blocked or stored up emotions, or soul wounds. Once you heal a chronic illness on the energetic level, it will begin to respond favorably to treatment on the physical level. Some will experience instantaneous healing, and sometimes it can take several months or even a few years for this to manifest in the physical. I was fortunate enough to get by without surgery on my eyes after these two eventful Constellations. Seekers are often led to the best source of healing for their chronic illness after their Constellation, because now it has been dealt with on an energetic level.

CASE STUDY #5
MY NINE-YEAR-OLD SON WAS ASKING
FOR THE FATHER HE'D NEVER MET

Sherry was overly concerned about her son's behavior. In the past, Luke was close to her and communication between them was good. As he approached age ten, however, he was becoming closed off and eventually shut down to his mother. Sherry did not know if kids were bullying him at school, or if another trauma had happened that changed his personality.

Family History: When I asked about her son's father, Sherry said Luke had never known his dad because her son was the product of a one-night stand. When she called and told his father, he refused to believe the child was his. She said her son had been asking about his dad lately, but she kept telling him "it was too complicated." She explained that after that one encounter with him refusing to take any responsibility, Sherry's mother had talked her into keeping Luke's biological father's name off the birth certificate and leaving him out of his life. It all made it easy for Luke's father to remain voiceless and unidentifiable to him.

The Circle Revealed: Sherry's intention was to heal the relationship between her and her son, and to find out more information so she could become close to him again. Interestingly enough, Sherry's Representative was wearing a necklace with a cowboy boot that sparkled with diamonds. The message coming from her Representative was that Sherry had given her son's dad "the boot" emotionally—and tried to make it look like she was doing Luke a favor by putting the sparkle on the boot. The Representative said, "You are serving him a shit sandwich and expecting him to eat it!" In other words, Sherry was communicating that she was doing her son a great service in keeping him from his father, when actually she was taking away his choice and right to know his father. Her son was resenting her for it.

Resolution: Sherry realized that she had not been honest and open with her son, so he had emotionally shut down to her. She realized she had taken away his right to choose to know his father, and that it was affecting him more than she had ever anticipated. She grew to understand that her choices greatly affected her son, and she chose to be more conscious of them. By granting her son the right to know what had transpired between his father and her, he was able to have the power to determine his father's place in his own life.

Comments: When someone in a family system denies another person's existence, it may cause a disruption in that family; there can be a painful emotional void or even trauma from that disconnect, especially in the case of one's biological parents. Even through adoption, the biological parent must be acknowledged for giving birth. That gift of life deserves acknowledgment.

Here's an analogy that might further help you to understand what epigenetics is, as presented in Nessa Carey's *Epigenetics Revolution*, and why it can have such a great impact in your life with Family Constellations.. Think of the human lifespan as a very long movie. The cells would be the actors and actresses, essential units that make up the movie. DNA, in turn, would be the script — instructions for all the participants of the movie to perform their roles. Subsequently, the DNA sequence would be the words on the script, and certain blocks of these words that instruct key actions or events to take place would be the genes. The concept of genetics would be like screenwriting. Follow the analogy so far? Great. The concept of *epigenetics*, then, would be like directing. The script can be the same, but the director can choose to eliminate or tweak certain scenes or dialogue, altering the movie for better or worse. After all, Steven Spielberg's finished product would be drastically different from Woody Allen's for the same movie script, wouldn't it?

CHAPTER TWENTY

Calling You to Your Highest Purpose

Of all the healing modalities I have studied and been certified in, as well as interviewed others and their certifications, I have found no other modality that heals individuals and families as powerfully as Constellations. Believe me, I've been around the world, searching for the smartest, wisest, and best answers for myself, for my family, and for my clients, as well as the cultures and people with whom I have fallen in love and had the desire to help in finding answers for healing. Constellations, by far, are the most powerful tool I've been able to find.

I invite you to try it out. It doesn't matter what healing you've done before, and what you haven't dared to try. This is the one to invest in your time and money because it gets personal, specific results in each of the bodies of your existence: emotional body, physical body, mental body, and spiritual body. Even Leonardo Da Vinci knew this, as depicted in his powerful Vitruvian Man.

My team and I have now been called all over the planet to facilitate this powerful work. Below are some ways I can help you and your family – and even your community - to resolve deeply hidden issues.

AROUND THE WORLD CONSTELLATIONS:
WORKING WITH SHAUNA CUCH

Even before I was trained in Constellations, I enjoyed traveling and met amazing people. I was an entrepreneur of a food service business and won awards with my wine bar. However, as my path changed to specifically helping others heal, I have met amazing people and been immersed in many beautiful cultures.

When I lived on the Ute Native Reservation for six years, I joined my husband in pouring for his Sweat Lodge. In working among the Natives, I was privileged to discover the beauty of their nature that so often gets overlooked in a dominant culture. It was an experience of a different kind of power, one of connection to the earth, sky, and animals. In Guatemala I spent months with a Mayan Elder and his family. They taught me ancient, powerful lessons on Mayan spirituality, along with language skills to understand the purity of what I was learning. It was a very sacred experience for me, as I discovered many ancient truths from them.

As I was healing, I worked in Columbia under three gifted shamans, who supported my necessary and deep shadow work through a plant medicine we call Grandmother. I spent weeks in Cuba learning about their amazing medical system that is set up to heal rather than to keep people sick. In Costa Rica I personally met and shook hands with the president of the country, as well as dined with the former president of the nation, a country who boasts of seventy years without an army. Instead, they spend the money on education and have a 96% literacy rate, the highest in South America.

In New Zealand, I learned about the Maori education system, culture, and how hospitable they are to guests visiting their mauri. I was invited to give a presentation on equine-facilitated learning to a horse-healing festival. From there, I went to Australia to meet with a couple that I did my first Constellation with, where I participated in a training on Constellations using horses.

In each of these countries, I was able to work with large groups of families and tribes. I have discovered two things I would like to share:

1. Every culture has knowledge and tools we can learn from.

2. Every culture and family system can benefit from Constellations. There is not one culture who has not suffered brutality, war, violence, sexual shame, and more on some level or another. As humans, we are learning, but these patterns have continued to be perpetuated. I feel the urgency to teach this in other lands, among many cultures, communities, and families. I also learned that Bert Hellinger, the original trainer and founder of Family Constellations, first learned the methodology from the Zulu people in Africa. I feel obligated to give them the recognition for impacting my life.

3. If you feel called to Family Constellations and believe Family Constellations with or without Equine Therapy would help you, your family, your culture, and civilization, I invite you to listen to the testimonials from others. I am very passionate about how fulfilling and deep this work is. I am happy to come to your community and facilitate.

I know that many people are not able to travel to me when it involves an entire family, or perhaps a group of people in conflict. The same is sometimes true for a jointly owned community or a nonprofit organization. Any group that is in need of healing or setting up a foundation of policies and procedures will benefit from Constellations as the patterns come forth objectively, without taking sides. As a world facilitator of Constellations, I delight in meeting new people in new places. I love serving families or community that need resolution or answers. It requires at least fifteen committed participants. Please note, if it involves another language, a translator will be necessary.

BUSINESS CONSULTING CONSTELLATIONS

If you are in a miserable working environment, it's important to note that you can heal the energy that has created the conflict. Also, if you are a CEO, we do business Constellations to energetically work out the issues. For example, if you are not profitable, we can find solutions for making your business profitable. If you are thinking about investing and want more insight on the integrity or intention of the investors or the property, you would be amazed at the answers that come from the Knowing Field. In Germany where this method began, it is common practice to use Constellations for engineering of any kind. Why not follow the wisdom of truth?

DISEASE AND ILLNESSES ALL BEGIN ENERGETICALLY

If you or a loved one have either chronic or genetic diseases or illnesses, we can uncover the message that is stored or blocked in the body that needs to be heard. Most often they are passed on from ancestral patterns, especially for a child inheriting a disease. An article in the Washington Post on December 7, 2013 by Meeri Kim, tells about an experiment with mice and cherry blossoms that shows the trauma from fear was passed on to six generations. The growing field of epigenetics is shining a light on the impact of ancestral trauma on the health and well-being of current generations.

GRIEF FROM DEATH

If you have someone dear to you that has passed on and you feel incomplete with their passing, you can resolve unspoken issues with the healing that takes place in the circle. This has been known to be extremely valuable in processing grief.

ABANDONMENT/ADOPTION/ABORTION/HIDDEN DEATH

Everyone belongs to a family system they chose. When they are denied that right to exist by any kind of conflict or circumstance, the energy from that will be persistent enough to keep showing up from generation to generation until it is resolved. Many times there is a lot of shame around the death of a child. Their name is never spoken of because of these circumstances, that will keep manifesting themselves. Any one of these issues can cause a very deep fracture in the family system that will continue to show up until it is resolved. Many times, this fracture shows up in dysfunctional relationships through projection onto one's partner.

Adopted children belong to the family system they were born into energetically, so they would need to do the healing for abandonment on their biological ancestral line as well as putting in their adopted family. If they have come from traumatic circumstances such as severe addiction, this trauma will show up sooner or later in their lifetime or their posterity. It is vital to do the work to release the patterns.

WORLD ISSUES AND MIGRATION TRAUMA

Each country had a different vibration. Many times, one who has migrated from their country feels as if they were abandoned by their mother. We have put migration issues into the circle and found it to be very successful and effective. The Seeker can speak their language and get complete. We have also helped some get their work permits in America.

GENDER CONFUSION

Many have difficulties accepting their body or their preference, whatever the case may be. Constellations can help them come out with ease and grace. Not all gender confusion is natural; some children have inherited a deep rage or resentment for the opposite gender and don't realize it does not belong to them. For some, it is completely natural, and Constellations break down barriers of judgement inside the self and help release judgement of yourself and others forward and back. I have done some very successful healing in this area.

TYPES OF CONSTELLATIONS

There are many other kinds of Constellations that include animal Constellations, ecological Constellations, nature Constellations, world peace Constellations, and more. First we invite you to join our conscious community where you will be welcomed by many people who have done their inner work and are supporting you in your journey to be the best version of your Self.

HERE'S WHAT WE ARE OFFERING:

- Conscious Community Membership
- Coaching packages that include men only, women only and combined group interaction with Conscious Community
- Relationship Alchemy (guaranteed to raise the bar in your relationships to bring more love, money, open communication and intimacy, and deeper self-love)
- Ancestral Healing Package
- Personal Challenges/Intensive Inner Work retreat
- Dynamics and Differences of Men/Women 101 virtual seminars (for couples and parents)
- Sovereign Relationship (Must have Relationship Alchemy completed)
- Parenting with Partnership Virtual seminars
- Eternal Call of the Soul virtual seminars
- Feminine Divine Retreat (Must have prior ancestral work done)

- Masculine Divine Retreat (Must have prior ancestral work done)
- We also host vacation retreats that include daily Constellations, tours, healing modalities, etc.

Go to www.journeyintotheheart.net to learn more. If you feel led to sign up now and mention this book, you will receive a special discount for our next ancestral package, a free master class that includes a bonus one on one call from the relationship expert!

Journey into the Heart Workshops

Text (801) 651-0539

Or email shauna@journeyintotheheart.net to answer any questions you might have.

Check out the testimonials on our website at www.journeyintotheheart.net

ABOUT THE AUTHOR

S hauna is an expert at helping you take a deep dive into self-love so you can love more fully. She researched over 100 men and taught over 200 women, all while earning her qualifications to help understand the subtle differences between men and women. She is also a coach in communication courses and a sought-after business consultant. In the latter capacity, she brought seven businesses out of the red and tripled their profitability. Shauna is known for leading events that deepen your awareness to find the communication skills of emotional sovereignty.

Shauna brings a unique mix of genuine and inclusive ancient healing-wisdom traditions and rituals to her method for healing relationships.

She was raised in an oppressive polygamous group and she has a lot to offer, having faced many challenges as one of four wives. Shauna is the mother of 11 successful children who make huge contributions to the world. Widowed at 42-years-old with six children still at home and only a tenth-grade education, she started a catering, restaurant-café and wine bar that won several awards. She was nominated for and won Mother of the Year from the Governor of Utah. However, when it was discovered she was a polygamous wife, she was not given the award. The successful HBO series, *Big Love* referenced that incident.

Her methods are widely used in numerous countries that value the work of Family Constellations and Systemic Healing. Her wisdom and use of a wide variety of specific and dynamic modalities raise the vibration, frequency, and consciousness in any circle. Her approach is unique, individualized, and draws on her years of experience, not only in Constellations, but in Shadow Clearing, which is the practice of transmuting darkness to light within our divine energy fields.

Shauna is the CEO and Founder of Journey into the Heart. She leads a phenomenally successful course called Relationship Alchemy, which helps you find peace of mind amid the chaos and provide the soul with sovereignty in any given situation. She helps people in toxic relationships to uncouple in a way that relieves pain and avoids unnecessary drama and expense.

www.JourneyIntoTheHeart.net

Facebook: JourneyIntoTheHeart

Instagram: journeyintotheheart7

LinkedIn: Shauna Cuch

REVIEWS

"*Big Souls Make Big Promises* is an extraordinary, healing methodology book. Shauna gives a tremendously powerful peek into healing significant intergenerational trauma, using her discovery of family constellation healing combined with equine therapy. She does so against the backdrop of her own extraordinary story.

"Shauna not only healed herself and her children from the deep wounding of polygamy, including physical, and spiritual abuse, but provides powerful case studies to illustrate the healing work of individuals from a wide array of backgrounds. This book will open your eyes to the vital importance of healing generational trauma. A five-star work!

   —Bridget Cook-Burch, New York Times Bestselling Author & Mentor
   www.YourInspiredStory.com

"This book provides a glimpse into the deep and sometimes dark parts of the soul that we have all come here to recover. As a holistic educator and spiritual guide, I have a keen interest in the subject matter and was fascinated by both the unusual lifestyle perspective as well as my first introduction to the amazing synthesis of equine therapy and family constellation work to lead us to the innate truth of energetic patterns. Brilliant! This rich tapestry weaves the author's personal stories and diverse life experiences with practical case studies to offer the reader a taste of the divine connection that runs through us all. What a gift to devote yourself to healing these unhealthy family patterns so that more soul's on the planet can flourish and be set free. Well done!"
—**Aeriol Ascher, MsD**
www.AeriolAscher.com

"A guide to know thyself better... *Big Souls Big Promises* tells us about the family that lives in us. With powerful testimonies, Shauna invites us to reflect on our bonds of attachment, visible and invisible, and on the script of life that we strive to live, sometimes against our authentic dreams ...

Who chooses me when I choose? Who really owns this life I'm living? These questions tell us that our freedom to live is not always complete.

This book is a treasure of consciousness to embody our authentic Self. Francesco di Castri said "You can't have wings until you have roots", and Shauna is taking us to our roots in order to really fly."

> **—Sophie Roumeas - Therapist, coach in mindfulness and French writer**
> **Mindful Therapies (Hypnosis & Systemic Constellation)**
> **www.sophieroumeas.com**

"I found the articulation of the events leading up to your current work as a Constellations Coach very heartfelt and filled with healing intentions and kindness. I am certain your clients have benefited not only from the wisdom you have received in your life as a result of your own traumas, but also from the goodness and healing effect in your sweet soul. Reading your book reminded me of a quote from the philosopher Friedrich Nietzsche, "A bad conscience is the pregnancy through which one must pass in order to be reborn into beauty." The early experiences of your clients, as well as those in your own life, suggest that you truly have facilitated transformational moments, not only in their lives, but also, and especially, in your own. This is a good thing! We can always respond in a much more life-supporting manner to whatever has happened to us in the past and your coaching is crucial in this regard! Your book is from the heart and reflects an honesty and a compassion rare in this world. Congratulations on a life well lived!"

—Randall Tolpinrud, President Pax Natura Foundation
http://www.paxnatura.org/

Shauna gives voice to that inner child we all have inside who craves to be loved, nurtured, and listened to as part of a family and the world we share. No one should have to demand to be heard in a world that often finds value in silence, conformity, and under the control of others. Join Shauna on her journey in learning how to trust herself and others to understand her place in the world.

—Dr Cheryl Lentz, TEDx Speaker & #1 International Best-selling Author
www.DrCherylLentz.com